Emotional Fitness

For my beautiful Barbara
thank you for always being there

Emotional Fitness

Facing yourself, facing the world

Cynthia Morton

Foreword by Dr Timothy Sharp

FINCH PUBLISHING
SYDNEY

Emotional Fitness

This edition first published in 2004 in Australia and New Zealand by Finch Publishing Pty Limited, PO Box 120, Lane Cove, NSW 1595, Australia. ABN 49 057 285 248

06 05 04   8 7 6 5 4 3 2 1

National Library of Australia Cataloguing-in-Publication entry
    Morton, Cynthia J.
    Emotional fitness: facing yourself, facing the world.

    Includes index.
    ISBN 1 876451 58 0

    1. Self-actualization (Psychology). 2. Emotions. 3.
    Self-defeating behavior. 4. Self-acceptance. 5. Victims -
    Psychology. I. Title.

    155.25

Edited by Kathryn Lamberton
Editorial assistance from Rosemary Peers
Text designed in Cheltenham by saso content and design
Typeset by J&M Typesetting
Cover design by saso content and design
Cover photograph courtesy of Dick Marks
Internal photographs courtesy of Douglas Watkin, Double Wire Productions
Printed by Southwood Press

Notes The 'Author's notes' section at the back of this book contains useful additional information and references to quoted material in the text. Each reference is linked to the text by its relevant page number and an identifying line entry.

Disclaimer While every care has been taken in researching and compiling the information in this book, it is in no way intended to replace professional advice and counselling. Readers are encouraged to seek such help as they deem necessary. The author and publisher specifically disclaim any liability arising from the application of information in this book.

Other Finch titles can be viewed at **www.finch.com.au**

155.25
MG46e

Contents

Foreword

When I first heard Cynthia speak, at a conference in Sydney at which I too was speaking, I was, to be perfectly honest, incredibly impressed. Her raw, gut-wrenching honesty was immensely moving and to some extent caught me by surprise in the context of what was essentially an 'academic' meeting of health professionals.

During one of the breaks in the meeting I introduced myself and almost immediately raised the idea of writing something together. This was not typical for me as Cynthia was (and is) not the sort of person with whom I had previously collaborated. That is, she didn't have a degree in psychology, nor for that matter did she have a degree in any related discipline. In fact, as impressed as I was with her presentation, I was also somewhat confused by the language she used which was, to put it bluntly, not at all like the language I was used to.

Never, for example, had I read in any psychology text descriptions of different people as 'dolphins' and 'sharks'. Being academically trained and a proud sceptic, I normally would have questioned the validity of such descriptors, but there was something about the way Cynthia used the language she used (and the language she uses in this book) that made it sound quite appropriate and accurate.

I subsequently got to know – and to like and admire – Cynthia better; and several subsequent conversations, as well as readings of her other writings, led me to gain a better understanding (and respect) of the 'program' she'd developed to help others overcome some of the problems she faced in her life. Although I was not previously a believer in the approach that advocated survivors were the best helpers, in Cynthia's case I believe she has an enormous amount to offer many people (and hopefully that includes you).

The basic principles she describes in this very personal 'self-help manual' are similar in many ways to the proven strategies I daily teach clients in my practice. As such, it was with considerable pleasure that I contributed to this book and it is with just as much pleasure and pride that I provide this foreword. I hope you enjoy the following pages and that you use Cynthia's Emotional Fitness program to train yourself and to achieve greater happiness.

Dr. Timothy J Sharp
Founder and Managing Director
The Happiness Institute

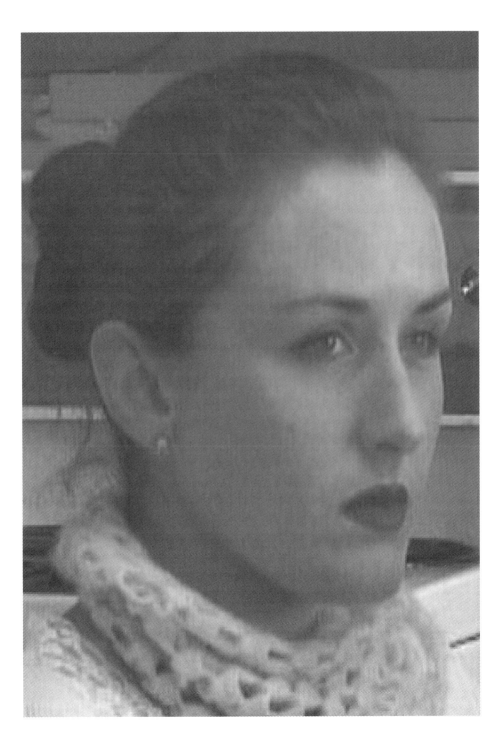

Preface

I chose to create the emotional fitness workouts in this book because I was so tired of editing myself, feeling less than other people and worrying about what they thought of me. I wanted to know how not to abandon myself when others in my life did. I deeply desired to become emotionally strong, unafraid of my feelings, my truth and any changes that life threw at me.

Building emotional fitness takes time, just as building physical fitness does. As physically fit bodies take all sorts of external forms, for example, a marathon runner's frame will be different from a weightlifter's frame, the areas you focus your physical workouts on will depend upon what you want your body to be able to do. Emotional fitness workouts are no different. The emotional areas you work on the most will be where you will become the strongest. This will vary from person to person. And with each individual it will look different from the outside. For some people becoming emotionally fitter may mean losing weight, for others it may mean gaining weight; for some it may mean leaving a relationship, for others it may mean staying.

Emotional fitness is about being who you are and honouring and taking responsibility for that. It's about self-honour no matter what others may think. Being emotionally fit is not about having the external package perfect for the rest of the world to judge. It's not about being in a relation-ship or out of one, having kids, or not having kids. It's about having your internal world a safe and true place for you, so that being you becomes a pleasure and an adventure. They say that true happiness is found when you want what you have. What you have you are responsible for.

Honouring myself in the beginning felt awkward and wrong because emotional self-neglect had been my natural state for the first three decades of my life. But repetition and sticking at it have been the keys – it is common knowledge that what we hope to do with ease, we must first do with diligence.

If we live a life of martyrdom and sacrifice for those we love, we grow to resent them. It is often said that it is selfish to honour yourself, but I believe the reverse to be true. If maintaining a relationship means that either person has to 'people-please' and live a lie, then it also requires the people involved to abandon who they are and become someone they are not. Love surely means to be true to yourself, if nothing else.

It is also an essential component of emotional health to have safe people to share your reality with. This book talks about safe people being emotional dolphins and unsafe people, emotional sharks. We all have the capacity to help or hurt ourselves and others. Being aware of our own wounds and tending to them so that we heal gives us the capacity to be wonderful dolphins for others. It is helpful to remember – *hurt people hurt people.*

In this book you will also meet Dr Tim Sharp, a Consulting and Clinical Psychologist and a Clinical Lecturer at the University of Sydney. Tim's many years of experience and his professional wisdom are interwoven throughout the forthcoming pages.

I met Tim when we were both speaking at a conference in Sydney in 2002. I liked him immediately. He seemed around my age, and did not look like a shrink. He had a sense of fashion and style, smiled a lot when he spoke, and his energy was gentle. Even though he was speaking to a roomful of medical professionals during his keynote address, he was warm and very human. I could tell from his energy that he loved his wife and children; he was a safe man, a human being first and a doctor second.

When we both sat together in a question panel at the end of the conference I noticed that many of our answers dovetailed. We were on the same frequency about emotional health and the recovery process. Tim too was already a published author and later spoke to me about his idea of writing a book like this. We were both enthused about the concept of a professional like Tim and someone like me who had been extremely emotionally unfit in the past contributing to one book written from both Australian male and female perspectives.

As you read these workouts and share my life's journey and Tim's helpful comments, our hope is that you will open not only your heart but also your mind, and perhaps not judge yourself and those around you so readily.

The hardest work we ever do is to honour ourselves consistently throughout life. It's an emotional marathon. But with the right preparation and training program we can not only weather all of the emotional seasons that life brings, we can also learn to see beauty and find peace in every emotional winter, spring, summer and autumn we encounter over the years.

Note: The photos in this book depict scenes from the Emotional Fitness program.

What is emotional fitness?

1

My husband kissed me on the forehead and quietly said, 'I'm too tired tonight, sweetheart, I just want to hold you and go to sleep.' A balanced, healthy sex life was something I had craved all my life, but I did not realise it would take so much emotional maturity to cope with.

This is my second marriage and I am now a mother of two teenage sons heading towards my forty-first birthday. I have been in therapy for six years.

My first marriage spanned nine years and, as with any past relationship, taught me a great deal about who I am and who I am not. I thought in those years that sex was my duty as a woman and that I had a quota I had to reach on a weekly basis. My first husband never said no, and I rarely did either, for it always triggered resentment and often a fight. I used to use sexual attention to validate my worth as a woman; I was like a drug addict. A flirtatious look from a stranger would give me a sudden rush. How things have changed!

As I nestled my head against my husband's warm, sleepy chest, I kissed him near his heart and said, 'I'll save it up for you when you are not so tired. Goodnight sweetheart, I love you.'

That is just one example of my level of emotional fitness today – not to sulk or get resentful, but to be able to honour and respect my husband and others when they say no to me. This used to be a huge emotional workout for me years ago but, gradually, by using the simple exercises in this book repeatedly, I have become emotionally fitter.

To be emotionally fit means to be unafraid of being yourself – warts and all! To build and maintain a loving and caring relationship with yourself – to be able to experience any emotion without needing to control it, suppress it, chemically enhance it or blame someone else for it – is the hardest work we ever do in our lifetime.

It is also an ability for self-preservation, an ability to remain flexible so that you can accommodate change without too much stress, but most of all, an ability to be brave enough to be vulnerable.

Self-acceptance is the by-product of emotional fitness – to be able to embrace the differences between yourself and others without making them or you feel superior or inferior. It's also about befriending the uncool person within you who holds all of your gifts.

At its elite level, emotional fitness means self-honesty in preference to vanity – in other words, humility. As the truth is neither convenient nor packaged in a way that your ego expects, emotional fitness calls upon your decency and your ability to be gentle with yourself and others. The workouts in this book are tough, but the reward is peace within your own head and heart – life's only true wealth.

Physical fitness and emotional fitness – similar principles

We all understand what it means to be physically fit or unfit, that all humans operate at differing levels of physical fitness, and that whatever level we choose we are responsible for. It is also common knowledge that a person's level of physical fitness dictates their physical quality of life.

On a scale of one to ten, one being the lowest or extremely physically unfit and ten being the highest or the level of an Olympian or an elite athlete, what number are you?

Me, I'm about a six, a little above average, but not much. And I accept I am responsible for that and comfortable with my current level.

Now, if I were to ask you, on the same one to ten scale, what your level of emotional fitness would be, could you come up with a number? If so, what is it? Do you know yourself well enough emotionally to evaluate your fitness level?

Let's say that you are totally emotionally unfit. You're unable to like yourself or anyone else long-term and having relationships seems impossible. The middle scale of five is average – you're able to hold a relationship but you're not as fit as you would like to be at the tougher emotional challenges, such as saying sorry, asking for help, resolving problems without holding a grudge and believing in yourself. Now we will look at the person who sits up at around nine to ten – those people who live in harmony with themselves and others 90 percent of the time. They don't let life get them down for long and they focus on problems as opportunities to find solutions.

My emotional rating today sits at about eight most days. During premenstrual times, my tolerance level plummets and I go down to a five or a six. However, the days are now increasing in my life when I feel I hit a nine and sometimes even a nine and a half.

When I began my recovery in 1995 I was about a one and a half to a two. I found life very overwhelming and simple everyday emotions very difficult for the first few months, and I could not work out why. Eventually, it came to me … I was emotionally very unfit, and I was responsible for that.

It made sense to me that if we could be either physically fit or unfit, then the same principle could apply to emotions: we could also be emotionally fit or unfit. And the level of our emotional fitness would dictate our emotional quality of life.

It is a physical law that nobody questions. If you exercise approximately three times a week for a minimum of half an hour and eat a balanced diet, you will maintain a level of physical fitness. However, if you exercise every day and eat a balanced diet, you will increase your fitness level. Input equals output.

So the conclusion I drew was that if I emotionally exercised I would become emotionally fitter, and that the more I did it, the fitter I would become. However, I needed help – an emotional personal trainer to help me untangle what was a healthy exercise and what was not, for I was very confused. Anything that meant being nice or generous towards myself felt wrong and selfish. I knew I was emotionally unfit but I was unsure how to fix it. I did not understand why I felt what I felt and sometimes emotions I felt had no name; they were just deep and overwhelming. I also was aware that I would need to commit to being emotionally fit if I were to get results.

I decided to do some work at home on my own, not just during my meetings with my personal trainer, so that I could build my emotional strength quickly. I felt so emotionally fragile and weak, and as a single mother on a pension with two young sons in the early days of my recovery, I needed all the strength I could possibly get as soon as possible.

The workouts within this book are for you to do on your own, as little or as often as you wish. Whether you work with or without a personal trainer is up to you. An emotional personal trainer could be a social worker, counsellor, psychologist or psychiatrist.

Alternatively, a trusted person to whom you can tell anything would also be able to assist you while you work out emotionally. I call these trusted people 'dolphins'. A dolphin is someone who inspires you, who leads by example – a doer not a talker. You could even call them a mentor if you like. Having both a personal trainer and a dolphin is ideal as this will help you get the quickest results. Dolphin people are not what I refer to as personal trainers as they don't have the same qualifications, but more about dolphins in the next chapter.

Notes from Tim Sharp

Most readers are probably familiar with the basic ideas of physical fitness and health referred to by Cynthia. The past few decades have seen an explosion of interest in, and availability of information on, diet and nutrition, as well as activity and exercise. Although we still have a long way to go, I would like to think that we are, as a society, more aware of and hopefully moving closer to being healthier.

Unfortunately, however, although the increased attention paid to diet and exercise is ultimately aimed at improving health and wellbeing, much of the literature and many of the proponents of this 'wellness' movement have ignored a large and significant range of contributing factors – psychological variables.

The psychological aspects of health and wellbeing include domains such as emotion and cognition. In addition to what we eat, and whether or not we exercise, the way we feel and the way we think are also important to our health. Cynthia's concept of 'emotional fitness' touches on this vitally important area and impressively describes, from the perspective of someone who's 'walked the walk', what it is like to identify a lack of 'fitness' and then to develop greater emotional strength.

In many ways, Cynthia's emotional fitness is similar to (although not exactly the same as) a construct that has been referred to as 'emotional intelligence'. According to one of the most influential writers in this area, Dr Daniel Goleman, emotional intelligence is 'the capacity for recognising our own feelings and those of others, for motivating ourselves, and for managing emotions well in ourselves and in our relationships'.

From my wider readings in this area, as well as my experiences seeing thousands of clients who have commonly been 'unfit', emotional intelligence can actually be broken down into several components:

- the ability to be aware of and to label or recognise our own emotions
- the ability to manage, or accept when necessary, our own emotions
- the ability to recognise others' emotions
- the ability to respond appropriately to others' emotions.

Cynthia will be addressing these and other related issues in more detail throughout this book but, for now, I would like to emphasise two more important points about emotional fitness. First, as Cynthia so rightly points out, developing your emotional fitness involves accepting responsibility in much the same way you do with regard to your physical health (including nutrition and exercise). And second, taking responsibility and actively pursuing improvement in this area does not necessarily mean you have to do it all on your own. There are professional 'trainers' (such as clinical psychologists and psychiatrists) who can help you achieve your emotional goals in the same way a personal trainer can help you achieve your strength and physical goals.

So the challenge for you before you read the following chapters is to decide whether or not you want to take responsibility for improving your emotional fitness and then to decide whether you believe you can achieve this on your own or, alternatively, whether you require help. Resolving these issues might not be easy but it might help if you try to answer these questions:

- Why do I want to become more emotionally fit?
- What are the benefits (for me and those around me) if I can improve my emotional fitness?
- What do I need to do to improve my emotional fitness?
- Am I really prepared to do the hard work required?

Only you, the reader, can answer these questions, but it is important that you give careful consideration to these issues while (or preferably before) you read the following chapters.

Emotional sharks and dolphins

I was ten days clean and sober and felt like a raw nerve. I had kicked off my shoes and had my feet up on the chair. I was holding onto my knees for dear life. This women's support group was terrifying. I felt like I did not belong here or anywhere on the planet for that matter. And then she spoke:

'My name is Barb and I used to get drunk every evening after my son and husband had gone to bed.'

I was in shock. This elegant woman spoke for about five minutes telling deep, dark secrets that no woman had ever shared before in my presence. She was not quite as old as my mother, but at least ten years older than me. She spoke in colour from her heart, not in black and white from her head. My heart understood every word she said.

She was a size 14, which was a taboo size according to my mindset. At this point in my life I starved myself so that I remained a size 10. But she was beautiful. She was shapely, soft, feminine and very attractive. She radiated energy that was like a pink rose and freshly baked bread. She felt like home. The tears rolled down my cheeks with relief as I bathed in the sound of her voice as if relaxing in a warm bath.

After the meeting concluded, I remained in my chair as she remained in hers speaking to another woman. I was magnetically drawn to her, almost against my will. I so desperately wanted to put my head in her lap and have her stroke my hair and tell me that I would be okay. That beautiful, safe maternal energy that oozed from her I was so thirsty for.

She turned around and smiled at me. I cried and put my head in my hands. 'Would you like a coffee, love?' she asked gently. I nodded, sobbing with gratitude that she had noticed me. I was 33 years of age and had found my first dolphin woman.

Where do the terms come from?

I created the terms 'emotional shark' and 'emotional dolphin' a few years ago. I do some charity work for The Abused Child Trust in my hometown of Brisbane and it was at one of their Christmas parties that this idea came to me. These brave little children aged around three to five years who were in what I call 'abuse rehab' had grown up in unsafe environments emotionally, physically and sexually. Many of them had little faith in human beings, and I understood that. I too as a child had their history and did not like or trust big people.

As a little girl I decided that Mother Nature was to be my heart's parent because she was so powerful, beautiful and reliable. She was the only consistent safe force in my life. Every day there was oxygen for me to breathe, the sun rose and set, and the clouds, sparrows, stars and trees became personal friends.

I am dyslexic, and even though I have no problem writing I don't comprehend the written word very well and I don't process left-side brain functions or anything academically based efficiently. I have never been able to distinguish my left from my right and I have a few other odd things over which my brain seizes.

So when explaining feelings or situations I call on Mother Nature's systems a great deal, for they are simple and make sense to me. Looking into the faces of these little people who had lived in emotional war zones, the fact that people can be like sharks and dolphins seemed glaringly obvious to me.

I see many similarities between human beings and these aquatic creatures. Sharks and dolphins both have grey fins so if you try to judge which one is safe and which one is dangerous by looks alone you could be fooled. People are the same. Looks alone are not a reliable source of information. Even though we have heard the old saying, 'Don't judge a book by its cover', we still teach children and adults to do exactly that.

Films like *Star Wars*, *Lord of the Rings* and *Harry Potter* all illustrate clearly to the viewer that the bad guy looks different. You are able to pick them visually by their physical characteristics.

In the media, we are still told that the size of a man's muscles, the shape of a woman's body or the type of car they drive tells you all you need to know about them as people. Externals show the fin only and do not give you enough information about what lies beneath the surface.

So I use these terms a great deal throughout the book, for many people I have spoken to at workshops or presentations respond favourably to them. They understand immediately what I mean. Safe and unsafe people, they are everywhere, in every culture, the world over.

However, in my lifetime, the most dangerous shark and the most beautiful dolphin I have ever met have lived within me. And those I have worked with over the past eight years with these exercises have found the same for themselves. Their very best friend and their most damaging enemy have both been within them.

Emotional fitness is about understanding the shark and the dolphin within you and bringing about peace between them.

The head – your shark's home

For many people the head and the heart are often at war. One normally wins, but they rarely work together in harmony. Our shark operates within our thoughts or what we often call 'our head'.

Our head is where we store data, past and present information that we collect in the hope that it will make us wiser in the future.

The shark is, however, only half of the emotional fitness equation. For balance we need the other half, which is the dolphin. For those who don't know how to access their dolphin, the shark becomes the controlling influence in their lives – like living in a world with only darkness and no sunshine for balance. Without a dolphin we develop an ego, and emotional imbalance becomes a way of life.

What does 'ego' mean in the context of the emotional fitness workouts in this book? E stands for Easing, G stands for Grace, O is for Out. We get stuck in our ego when we are easing grace out of our lives.

What is grace? It means honour – to gently honour ourselves is an act of grace. So when we dishonour ourselves we get stuck in ego. Thinking we are better than or less than another is dishonouring ourselves. We may have more highly developed skills, gifts or talents than another but that does not make us a superior human being. It just makes our role in life different from theirs.

Mother Nature makes all species with differing traits. Look at dogs and flowers, for instance: a Great Dane is different from a poodle as a rose is different from a tulip. They create diversity and interest but it seems futile to rate a tulip as better than a rose or a Great Dane as superior to a poodle.

The shark's job is to collect information, catalogue it by fear and store it for us for future reference. It is a library of fear and the shark is the librarian. If used in conjunction with our dolphin, however, it is a very useful resource that helps protect us and not repeat mistakes later in life.

The shark collects a library of tapes that it begins recording in our childhood – tapes that record messages such as 'we are not good enough', 'we can't' or the 'but what ifs'. These tapes are all designed to challenge us. They are merely obstacles, like furniture in a dark room. When you consider all of the people involved in our lives on primary, secondary and tertiary levels, many people's fears are passed on to us in our formative years. By the time we hit our teens, and eventually adulthood, the shark's tape library is diverse. And on cue the shark plays the fear-based tapes in our heads any time we try to grow and need to check out the danger factor in the risk we are about to take.

The shark acts as our rear vision mirror. Like when we're driving a car, it helps us when we need to merge, reverse or take a few steps back (this is often necessary when we are lining ourselves up to kick a goal in life), or to check who is following us. If we spend the whole time when driving our car looking in the rear vision mirror we miss what is in front of us and will inevitably crash. Fear is a reference point to help us check for safety and to learn how to self-preserve and take risks.

The shark or our fear is designed to challenge us, not control us. Problems arise for people who have not activated their dolphin to remind them that the shark is merely a checking resource. People without a developed dolphin often believe the shark's tapes as their truth. They have no other resource to shine a light on the shark's valuable darkness. When you have a torch to shine in a dark room you can work out what to avoid; without a torch you will hurt yourself. The dolphin is the torch.

We need the dark and the light: hot and cold, night and day, pain and love. One without the other has no meaning. The shark gives our lives meaning. It is not the enemy – merely a reference point.

Sharks and dolphins cohabit in harmony in the oceans and have done so for aeons. It is also nature's intention that they operate within us harmoniously.

The shark lives within us all. We can call it by many names: the dark, the shadow, the ego, the self, or fear. It is a necessary part of the human condition. It gives us a reference point. As Helen Keller put it, 'How could we learn how to be brave and patient if there were only joy in the world?'

The heart – your dolphin's home

The heart is where we store feelings, past and present emotions that we collect over the years in the hope that they will make us wiser in the future. Our dolphin operates within our feelings or what we often call 'our heart'.

The dolphin is the other half of the emotional fitness equation. It is the librarian of our love and hope tapes. Problems arise for people for whom dolphins were scarce in primary, secondary and tertiary relationships during childhood. The result is an adult with a vast range of shark tapes but very few dolphin tapes to help counteract their fears.

When we are in dolphin mode, we live, love, hope and radiate a sense of wellbeing and inner calm. We can laugh and shed tears; we feel alive and connected to other human beings. In a nutshell, we care about ourselves and each other. When children are surrounded by adults with active dolphins, they record these messages of hope and positivity for later use.

A dolphin is a master at self-preservation because it works in conjunction with the shark. It understands clearly that the shark is a valuable ally that helps us make wise decisions. A dolphin is neither a doormat nor a yes person, but an individual with healthy personal boundaries who is responsible for him- or herself.

People in life are like dishes on a smorgasbord. Some our palate enjoys; others it does not like. If we don't like liver, it does not make liver bad and us superior; it just means that our individual taste buds do not respond well to liver's taste. People are the same. Some personalities will not connect with ours. It is not about being better or worse, just different. To be at peace with our differences is how our dolphin can assist us in life.

Emotional fitness is quite simply about the head and the heart working together without one ruling the other so that we can live a balanced and fulfilling life.

Notes from Tim Sharp

In this chapter Cynthia refers to the emotional sharks and dolphins within and outside each of us. That is, every one of us has an internal shark and dolphin (in our head and our heart, according to Cynthia's model). At the same time, every one of us comes in contact with other people who may be more shark or more dolphin.

The challenge raised by Cynthia in this chapter is to learn how to identify the sharks and dolphins both within you and within others.

In professional psychology circles, Cynthia's concept of emotional sharks and dolphins is similar to what have been labelled automatic negative thoughts (or ANTs) and positive enabling thoughts (PETs). These concepts are derived from a therapeutic approach known as 'cognitive therapy' which, in brief, emphasises the importance of thoughts in determining how we feel and what we do. Essentially, the principal assumption of cognitive therapy can be summed up as 'you are what you think'.

In my experience, once people learn how to become *more aware* of their thoughts (both negative and positive) they are well on their way to learning how to *control* their thinking which, in turn, enables them to control (at least partly) how they feel. This is the essence of cognitive therapy and, to a large extent, of Cynthia's model of emotional fitness. So how do you do this?

To begin with, one of the strategies I have found most helpful with my clients (and I know Cynthia found this helpful too) is to start by keeping a 'diary' of how you feel and what thoughts go through your mind, particularly in certain situations. This is a relatively simple process that can be completed in different ways.

A simple formula, however, is to take a piece of paper, or a small notebook, and draw two vertical lines down the page forming three columns. At the top of the first column write 'situation'. At the top of the second column write 'emotions'. And at the top of the third column write 'thoughts'. All you need to do then is to fill in these columns whenever you have the chance.

At the very least, I recommend that you complete the 'form' two to three times each day. Typically, most people find it most helpful if they complete the form during times when they're distressed or feeling they are not coping as well as they would like. Any time you feel like this, write down (1) what you are/were doing, (2) how you feel/felt and (3) what thoughts are/were going through your mind.

Remember, the goal here is primarily to increase your awareness of how you feel in certain situations, not necessarily to make any changes yet. Learning to identify when your dolphin and shark is more active is, in many ways, a skill. And the more you practise the skill of awareness, the better you'll get. Further, the more aware you become, the more empowerment you will eventually gain.

This exercise can also be used to learn how to identify whether others are sharks or dolphins. If you feel uncomfortable in someone else's presence, use a similar form to describe the situation you were in and how you felt. Then ask yourself, 'What is it this person is doing (or does) that makes me feel uncomfortable?'

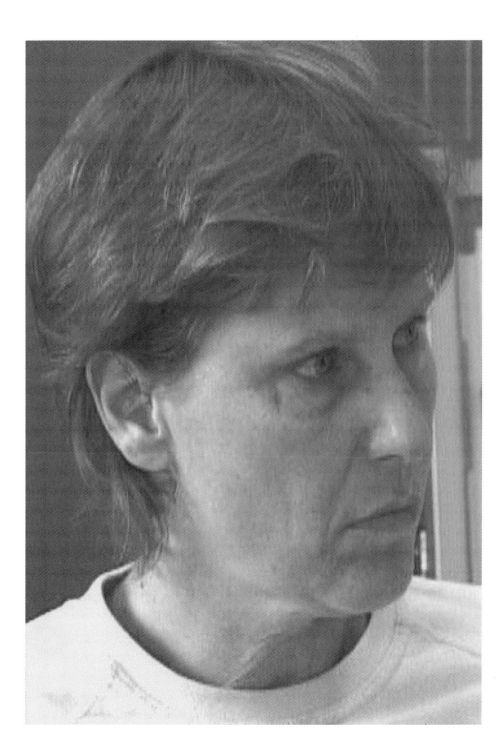

3 Beginner, intermediate and advanced workouts

We all have different types of relationships, depending on how close we are to the other person and what role he or she plays in our lives. So we need different types of workouts to suit these relationships.

What are primary, secondary and tertiary relationships?

These three types of relationships are best remembered by thinking of your school years. As a child, you learn first about primary relationships. These are the first relationships you are introduced to. Even if parents are absent, a child will form a primary relationship with their caregiver. Primary relationships involve a high level of vulnerability and that is what makes them so beautiful and yet so difficult at times. The quality of the primary relationships we have as children becomes our blueprint or emotional map for the future. We measure all other relationships against it.

If you think of a child starting primary school on the first day, the relationship they develop with their teacher is primary. There is vulnerability involved. They sometimes hold the teacher's hand, and may even freely have a cry with the teacher if they are upset. Their heart or dolphin is involved in the relationship. The heart/dolphin rules a child until they learn about the head/shark. I believe we are all born dolphins, and that it is a human's natural state. Fear or shark talk is learnt. A friend who has been blind since birth once told me that humans are born with only two instinctual fears. One is the fear of falling and the other is the fear of loud noise; every other fear is learnt.

Secondary relationships and secondary school have a lot in common. There is less emotional involvement, still some, but less than at primary school. The relationship with a teacher in secondary school or high school is not as involved as it was at primary school. The teacher only knows what we want them to know; we become more emotionally guarded through puberty.

Tertiary relationships are like tertiary teachers. We are not as emotionally affected by a teacher or lecturer at university as we were at primary or secondary school. We tend to get along with tertiary teachers better than with teachers in our past schooling life, as emotional heart contact with teachers has decreased a great deal by adult life. As the element of vulnerability diminishes, the easier the relationship becomes.

The beginner workout aims to help you relate to the tertiary people in your life; the intermediate is designed to help you with your secondary relationships; and the advanced workout aims at improving your relationships with the primary people in your life.

Beginner workouts in tertiary relationships

The following story shows that it is possible to relate assertively, rather than passively or aggressively, with the tertiary people you encounter in your life.

Saying 'no' to the bossy woman at the uniform shop

It was a week before my son was due to start at a new school. He was aged twelve and very uncomfortable about this big change. I decided to organise all his uniforms the week before so that on his first day he would be wearing the appropriate clothes and feel more comfortable.

We made our way through the maze of buildings, stopping to ask students along the way how to get to the uniform shop. Eventually we found the crammed old classroom that was stacked from ceiling to floor with uniforms. Socks, sports gear, shorts and hats lined every wall. In the corner was a makeshift dressing room with a very narrow curtain. The curtain was almost useless: there was a mother stretching the curtain out so that the little girl changing behind it had some privacy.

'Can I help you?' a woman asked impatiently from behind the cluttered desk. 'Yes, we need the whole uniform – shorts, shirts, socks, hat and whatever else is necessary. My son starts on Monday', I replied feeling like the new kid myself in this unfamiliar environment.

This school was in a more affluent suburb than my son's previous school and I immediately wondered if they knew I was not from the area. This was a strictly pearl necklace and European car neighbourhood and I had neither.

The woman scanned my son's body from head to toe and then proceeded to pull out shirts and shorts that she ordered him to try on in the dodgy fitting room. My son looked at me with pleading eyes not to have to undress and try on all these uniforms. 'Come on now, try these on, we haven't got all day, your mother needs to know if they fit', she demanded in a condescending tone.

'Mum, can we take them home and try them?' he asked in a whisper.

'For God's sake it'll only take a minute, come on now, we haven't got all day', the woman ordered him.

Prior to my recovery I would have wanted this woman to approve of me and to show her that my son would do as he was told. Worrying about what others thought of me, even strangers, really mattered. But now in recovery my priorities had changed. In my heart I wanted to put my son first before my ego and decided that this was a perfect opportunity to do an emotional workout.

'No, he is uncomfortable. We will take them home and try them on. I don't think we need to make this harder for him than it is already', I said as I looked the woman in the eye. I am sure my face went red and my heart was pounding but I was so pleased that I had said it.

'Of course, just bring them back if they don't fit.' To my surprise, the woman backed down completely. Bossy women like this had intimidated me in the past. I used to either retreat or attack them by becoming aggressive. I had never before asserted myself respectfully and said no.

My son looked at me with such gratitude and actually reached to hold my hand as we left the school. I had honoured myself and, as a result, I had honoured him as well. I am a grown woman. I did not want to be dictated to, but it was up to me to say so with the grace of a woman. I earned some self-respect that day and wrote about it that evening. It then became a dolphin record for me to use next time I needed to say no to a tertiary person.

Tertiary people in our lives

People who we are not deeply emotionally involved with are the easiest people with whom to start your workouts on emotional fitness. The relationships with these people are what I usually call 'surface' or 'tertiary' relationships.

We sometimes find that we tell these people things about ourselves that we are too guarded to tell those closer to us. We can flirt, share a joke, gossip and chat about the state of the world, and then go on our merry way. Tertiary relationships are often fun and easygoing, for they don't demand a great deal of emotional energy or vulnerability. Tertiary people usually only see us in our dolphin mode and it is a fact that positivity is contagious: dolphins generally bring out other people's dolphins. We see tertiary people from time to time, or sometimes during the weekly routine of our lives.

Tertiary people include:
- shop assistants
- waiters
- bar staff
- one night stands
- doctors
- mechanics
- hairdressers
- cab drivers.

It is with these people that I recommend you begin your emotional workouts. If you find any exercise too difficult at this level, don't attempt it at the intermediate or advanced level. I also strongly recommend you make sure that you are able to repeat the workout with ease at this level before you progress. Otherwise, you could hurt yourself or someone else and perhaps even do some serious emotional damage to yourself or the other person.

Intermediate workouts in secondary relationships

Once you have mastered the desired workouts at the beginner's level, you can move onto intermediate workouts with the secondary people in your life. These workouts are generally a little more difficult than those with tertiary people, mostly because there is some emotion involved in the relationship.

Saying 'no' to the old-timer at my recovery meeting

He had been in recovery for 25 years, and I had been clean and sober for five months. I was a shaking bundle of nerves. Drugs and alcohol had been my best friends for the past nineteen years. They did for me what relationships with people never had. They were always there for me and made me feel better for many years. It was my solution, but then it gradually changed and became my problem.

I was an emotional virgin and had no idea how to do life straight.

'Today I walk the streets with my head held high, I remember what I did yesterday and my family welcome me back into their homes with open arms', he said as he firmly placed his closed fist on the lectern in front of him.

I felt like I was in church – well I was in an old church hall and something about this man made him sound like a minister delivering the Sunday sermon. But he made me uncomfortable. He had one of those red, spongy, marshmallow-like noses that was swollen from years of drinking. He was in his sixties and wore his hair like the old movie stars used to. He introduced himself as an 'old-timer' and because of his clean time he automatically gained respect. I had heard his story many times, but something about him felt predatory and unsafe to me, and I felt guilty because I believed I was supposed to be in awe of him like everybody else. I was so afraid of honouring my truth because I was sure there must be something wrong with me for not thinking he was wonderful like everybody else.

'How are you, love?' he greeted me in the middle of the supermarket aisle as I shopped for the weekly groceries with my two sons, then aged nine and seven.

'Well, thanks', I answered, too scared to say that I was good because other people in recovery had said to me when I had said I felt good, 'Oh, it will pass', which had left me feeling low on hope. So I had learnt to reply that I was well, but not good.

He then went to pull me close to him and kiss me on the lips as he had done many times before, which had left me feeling like I wanted to scrub my skin clean. But for the first time, without thought, I held my hands out, palms facing him, giving him a clear stop signal. I did not like this older man assuming he could kiss me on the lips and pull me close to him whenever he chose just because he had been clean and sober longer than me. For some reason, having my boys with me I was less afraid and felt compelled to draw this boundary with him once and for all?

'No Doug, I'm not big on touch, I hope you understand', I said gently but firmly. He went red in the face like a young child being caught with their hand in the lolly jar.

'Righto', he muttered as I pushed the trolley past him taking my youngest son by the hand. I had seen this man weekly for five months and finally I had been able to speak up for myself. I had finally done it and I felt empowered.

Becoming used to saying no when necessary to people in my tertiary circle had given me the confidence to now assert myself responsibly with dignity in my secondary circle. I no longer felt I had to be, do and say what others wanted. This was the beginning of taking my power back; I began to feel I was living with the grace of a woman rather than the grief of a child.

Secondary people in our lives

Secondary relationships involve more frequent contact and a little more emotional input than tertiary relationships. Secondary people know us, but only what we want them to know about us. There is not a great deal of emotional vulnerability within these relationships and we tend to control their intensity. They are interesting relationships: sometimes we socialise with these people but keep up an emotional guard just the same.

Secondary people usually include:

- work colleagues
- sporting team mates
- social acquaintances
- old school friends
- fellow students
- recovery friends
- teachers
- recreational acquaintances (gym, yoga, dancing, bushwalking)
- parents of your children's friends
- your parents' friends
- children of your parents' friends
- your partner's friends
- next-door neighbours.

These people have more involvement in our daily lives and generally speaking we are destined to see them on a more regular basis than tertiary people.

Advanced workouts in primary relationships

When completing an emotional fitness workout with anyone in your primary circle it becomes an advanced workout. These are the hardest workouts because the emotional involvement is so deep. When vulnerability is a factor, people are easily wounded. Therefore, it is essential that emotional fitness is at an optimum before attempting these workouts, as you will see from the story below.

Saying 'no' to my mother

The fear of my mother being angry with me still niggles at me today as a 41-year-old woman, but it no longer controls me or creates the need to edit myself for her approval.

I was in very early recovery and was only just beginning to see how dysfunctional I had been over the past decades. As an active drug addict and alcoholic I used to pick my two sons up from school loaded with drugs and alcohol. My car would roar into the school car park with the stereo blaring so loudly that the car doors would vibrate. I would be singing to Whitney Houston at the top of my lungs as I slammed my foot on the brakes, parking over the line that separated the car parks and taking up two spaces.

In those days I figured that Pamela Anderson had the Barbie Doll look pretty much sown up so I modelled myself on her. I am 180 centimetres tall and weighed about 59 kilograms, but I was obsessed with being over-weight, so I starved myself and lived on laxatives. I wore my hair long and tussled trying to create that sex kitten look. As I staggered out of the car in high heels, my lolly pink miniskirt accidentally caught in my undies, my baby doll, low-cut top barely containing my newly enhanced breasts, cigarette in hand as if I were a movie star, I am sure I was an entertaining sight for the other mothers sitting quietly in their cars waiting to collect their children. I would stagger out of the car to try and find my two boys, winking at the school teachers in my path. My poor boys must have cringed, I am sure, as they saw their trashed mother approaching.

But things had changed. In early recovery I was able to sit in the car patiently like other mothers, but with such remorse at the memories of how I used to arrive at the school. At this time my beautiful boys would get into the car with warm smiles on their faces because their mother did not reek of alcohol and the car was not full of cigarette smoke. I started to notice little freckles on their noses that I had never seen before, we chatted about their day, and even though their father and I had separated they were more relaxed and affectionate.

My mother is a good woman. And I write about her with such a heavy heart. She was my favourite drinking partner, and we had a lot of fun. We cried together and laughed together; we went out on the town flirting and dancing. We were close, but alcohol was the thread. When I got clean and sober things were never the same.

In the first few weeks of my recovery, I remember being at my mum's house, sitting on the floor and hugging the dog I had just brought home from the dog refuge. She came and sat on the floor next to me. She had been drinking all afternoon and with cigarette in hand she put the arm holding the glass of wine around my shoulder so it sat just underneath my mouth. It was not an intentional tease on her part; she was genuinely trying to comfort me. But everything in my being was screaming so loudly for a cigarette and alcohol that I had to get out of there. I could not sit and watch her drink glass after glass any more. It made me very sad. Her words would start to slur and her personality would change. I started to understand what my boys had been witnessing when I used to drink myself into oblivion – I saw myself.

One afternoon, during the week following this awakening, Mum rang me and asked if she could pick up the boys from school and take them to her place. I knew she had just been to lunch and had been drinking. She, as I often had, drove after many glasses of wine. I knew she would be over the legal limit.

'I'll give them dinner to give you a break and you can pop over when you are ready', she said with care in her voice. My heart was pounding. I did not want the boys to be driven by her any more unless I definitely knew she had not been drinking. I started to sweat and the lump in my throat felt like a bowling ball.

'No, Mum', I said, and those words sounded like I had just announced that the world was going to end in five minutes. There was silence on the other end of the phone. I was shaking, and shocked that I had actually said it. Still silence.

'Why don't you come over here for dinner to see the boys? I'll pick them up, it's fine.' She knew my voice and must have picked up that those words were very difficult for me to say.

'Why can't I pick them up?' she demanded defensively. 'What's wrong with me picking them up?' she snapped.

'Mum, I would just prefer it if you came over to our house, I would feel more comfortable.' I was fighting back tears of fear; my voice was trembling.

I was also uncomfortable about male partners my mother had. Most of them were extremely heavy drinkers like my father was. I had been abused by two men as a child, sexually and physically – my father and the next-door neighbour. My mother's maternal radar did not function when she drank, which is a common problem for women drinkers, myself included. I had to make sure that my boys, aged seven and nine at that time, were safe now. I had been too irresponsible for too long.

'How dare you! I am their grandmother, it is my right. You have no right to deprive me of seeing my grandchildren. I have done nothing wrong. What have I done? I was a good mother!' She was on the attack. My heart was pounding so heavily I could almost hear it as tears rolled down my cheeks.

'Mum, you are welcome here any time. I am just not comfortable with the boys at your place without me there too now.' My voice quivered and perspiration streams rolled down my body.

'What's wrong with you? They are my grandchildren, what about them? You are going to screw them up – they want to see their grandma,' she dictated in that 'mother knows best' tone.

I could not tell her that the last time I left her with them they asked me not to leave them there again. When I collected them she had been drinking and they began to fight with each other because they were so upset. They did not want to go any more.

It was either betray my maternal feelings and my two young sons who had been through so much already, or betray her. It was the hardest no I have ever had to say in my life. But I said it, and can say no in primary relationships with more ease these days. I will never forget it, I was terri-fied – and I was 33 years old.

Primary people in our lives

Primary relationships fall into different categories: those we choose and those we are born or marry into. Those we are born into are often the most difficult because there is no conscious choice when we are children as to whether we want these people in our lives. We have to live with them. When we become adults we do have choices with these relation-ships. We can move away from those we are biologically related to if we decide to and if we are emotionally fit.

It is healthy for children to leave the family home, not just physically but emotionally as well. That is what makes the difference between a woman and a girl and a man and a boy. When a child can stand alone physically and emotionally from their parents and honour themselves they have become an adult. This entails being able to disagree and draw personal boundaries.

Many people physically leave home and even travel to the other side of the world but still obey their parents' (shark or fear-based) voices in their heads, unable to disagree without the guilt of feeling disloyal. A parent can be dead and buried and still the fear of emotional abandonment stifles the child's capacity to go against their parent's opinion.

Lovers who become partners and sometimes spouses are examples of primary people whom we choose. Many people say that their partners changed once they married or had children. Often what has happened is that their relationship has simply shifted from a secondary to a primary level. The vulnerability level increases at the primary level and if people find vulnerability difficult primary relationships will also be difficult for them.

Primary people include:

- yourself
- mother and father
- stepmother and stepfather
- grandmother and grandfather
- brother and sister
- stepbrother and stepsister
- foster parents
- husband and wife
- daughter and son
- boarding masters
- nuns and priests
- psychiatrists/psychologists/social workers/therapists and counsellors
- in-laws
- ex-partners
- intimate long-term partners/lovers/friends/housemates.

You will change emotionally in a healthy way if you commit to these workouts, just as you see healthy physical changes when you commit to consistent physical workouts.

When one individual in a primary relationship starts to emotionally work out and the other does not, the dynamics of the relationship inevitably change.

In some primary relationships, if one person starts to lead by example in reclaiming their life and personal power emotionally, the other becomes motivated to do the same. It happens often with physical fitness too. One person becomes fitter and the other follows suit, and they may even become running partners.

However, in some cases, if one person changes and the other does not, the dynamics that made the relationship function don't always continue to work. It is important to remember that being emotionally fit, as with being physically fit, does not make you superior, just different.

Some people who you least expect will become emotional running partners with you; others will not. These workouts will bring about change for the better for you, but it is important to understand that others may not wish to join you – live and let live is the best approach with these workouts.

Notes from Tim Sharp

In Chapter 2 Cynthia began to describe the first stage of an emotional fitness workout, which could be compared with undergoing a physical assessment to determine where you need to devote your time and your energy.

If you were to start training with a responsible personal fitness trainer they would begin with a brief review of your current condition. This would then shape the nature of your program and influence the extent to which you would focus on different domains of health, such as aerobic fitness, strengthening and flexibility.

Along similar lines, the exercises I recommended at the end of Chapter 2 are aimed at helping you identify your current level of emotional fitness and thereby beginning to recognise the areas on which you need to focus. For example, if after completing the thoughts and feelings monitoring form for a few days, you realise that you're feeling angry and frustrated much of the time, then this would become a pointer to where you could begin your workout.

In this chapter, Cynthia begins to describe the first steps of the emotional fitness workout and the challenge for you, the reader, is to begin to learn how to recognise when your thinking, feeling and reacting is unhelpful. In addition, the challenge of this chapter is to begin to think about what you can do to question or change your thinking, feeling and reactions if you believe them to be counterproductive or self-defeating.

Based on my readings of countless research papers and therapy books, as well as my extensive experience with a variety of clients, I suggest that the best place for those interested in taking this next step is to review their monitoring forms and then to start asking questions.

To begin with, it's important to realise that just because you think something, that thought is not necessarily true. Thoughts are not facts. In contrast, thoughts are often biased and distorted. This is not an intentional process, but it is a significant one, because if your thoughts are distorted in some way and if they're thereby causing distress, this distress may well be excessive and/or unnecessary.

The good news is that we can learn to 'correct' our thoughts by asking questions such as 'Is this really true?' or 'Is it helpful to look at this situation this way?'. Similarly, 'Is there another way I could view this situation/problem?' or 'How would someone else (for example, a dolphin) think about what's going on?'.

In very simple terms, if you find your thoughts are frequently biased (that is, too focused on negatives, overly black and white, excessively overestimating the chances of things going wrong, unnecessarily blaming yourself for things outside your control), then it's crucial you do whatever you can to replace them with more realistic, more helpful, more (in Cynthia's schema) dolphin-like ways of thinking. If you can do so, I can guarantee that you will feel considerably less distress and considerably more happiness and satisfaction.

This chapter points to the importance of reviewing not just what you say to yourself but also how you respond to and interact with others. In many ways, the principles are the same in that my suggestions to clients often involve recommending that they ask themselves very similar questions. However, instead of questioning their thoughts, I encourage them (and I now encourage you) to question the way they respond to others. For example, review several recent interactions you've had with others and ask yourself 'Was my response helpful?', 'Was what I did in my best interests?', 'Was there another way I could have reacted?' and 'Would this other interaction have been more consistent with the dolphin I want to be?'.

On this last point it is important that you have an image of what and who you want to be. If you don't know what you want to be and how you want to behave then it will be hard for you to achieve it. What helped Cynthia was to have a dolphin role model. Do you know anyone who could be your role model or mentor? If so, ask them for advice. If not, then maybe it would be worth seeking the help of a professional.

Finally, Cynthia makes a very important point in this chapter, which is that you should not try to do or change too much too quickly. If you want to start behaving differently in certain situations, that's great, but work up to it. Start with easier situations and more distant (or tertiary, in Cynthia's terminology) people and then only work your way up once you feel confident and comfortable. In the same way you would probably jog around the block before you entered a short fun run before you attempted a marathon, so too should you initially practise your assertiveness and other new behaviours on people more distant from you, and then build up to closer, more intimate relationships.

4 The elite emotional workout

I was having a fat and ugly day. My shark was playing very loudly within my head and I could not see anything good about myself. I was impatiently waiting for my turn to be served. The lingerie shop assistant must have been only about twenty years old. She was gorgeous too. As she twittered away in her sugary voice to the woman in front of me I assassinated her in my head. Her tiny hips and pert little bottom in tight-fitting black hipster pants looked great. She must be anorexic, I hoped to myself. But then her full peach-like cleavage bursting out of her lacy pink top looked natural and contradicted my starvation theory – definitely not implants. I was an expert on them, I decided, having had them myself.

'Sorry to keep you, madam, can I help you?' she asked, smiling at me as if I were her grandmother.

'I certainly hope so', I snapped. 'I am here to pick up a bra I ordered two weeks ago. They told me it would be here within a week, so it should be here', I said sternly, looking at her dead in the eye as if her overwhelming beauty had no effect on me at all.

At that point I wished that it was a gorgeous sexy bra I was picking up, but it wasn't. It was a sensible, maternal-looking beige one. I so wanted to appear worldly and more experienced than her, as my shark had convinced me that I had turned into a gross marshmallow in my late thirties.

'No, it's not back yet, madam ...', she went to explain as her perfectly manicured fingernail located my order in her book, but I interrupted her abruptly.

'What do you mean it's not back yet? I was specifically told that it would be here in a few days. I cannot come all the way back here again – it's not good enough. When will it be in – do you know that much?' I demanded condescendingly.

She became flustered, which pleased me in my bitchy, shark-like state and stuttered … I did not allow her to respond.

'This is bloody ridiculous, I haven't got time for this today', I snapped and stormed out of the shop.

I was riding the escalator to the upper floor of the shopping mall after my dramatic exit and began to feel a deep sense of disappointment in myself. What a bitch I had been! I had compared myself to that innocent young girl and emotionally dumped on her for my insecurities. I had done my morning warm-up and knew that these actions did not align with the woman I was choosing to become – a woman of grace and dignity, like my beautiful dolphin, Barbara, not a frustrated old witch. I knew what I had to do. I turned around at the top of the escalator and went straight back down to the lingerie shop level.

As I walked into the shop the young assistant took a deep breath and held onto the counter as if to brace herself for another onslaught from me. I walked straight up to her, grateful that the shop was empty of other customers.

'I am so sorry, I was such a bitch to you before. I was just in a savage head space. It was uncalled for, I know you were only trying to help me', I said, leaning over the counter gently touching her forearm as I spoke.

She let out a sigh of relief and her eyes smiled warmly at me.

'Thank you so much for that, I am new here and I am sorry if I kept you waiting too long. I will call and find out where your bra is and ring you as soon as it arrives … I really appreciate you coming back.'

My self-respect was back intact. My morning warm-up had helped me stay true to myself even when I made a mistake and let my shark, or fear, take control. For me, these days, emotional fitness at its elite level is being able to choose again if I make a mistake and put my dolphin back in charge of my day.

Peak performance

To attain elite levels of emotional fitness it is imperative not to cut corners or skip any of the steps suggested below, specifically warming up emotionally at the beginning of your day and warming down at the end of it.

Just as an elite physical athlete would never commence a workout without warming up their muscles first, it is a must that you warm yourself up emotionally before you start your day. Warm-down also plays a vital role in physical fitness as it allows the body to cool down and regain its balanced heart rate. The same principle applies to emotional fitness. Often after a challenging day an emotional warm-down helps us learn from our experiences, lower our heart rate, collate feedback and give ourselves credit for having a go at emotional fitness no matter what our day was like.

An Olympic athlete knows that their peak performance can only be reached after a warm-up. As a car's motor takes time to warm up before it can reach peak speed, so too do our physical and emotional motors. Cars often stall if the engine is not allowed to run before top speeds are demanded, and human muscles can be pulled and strained if warm-up stretches and exercises are not included in a physical fitness regime. The same principles apply to your emotional wellbeing. Without warming up and warming down, emotional stalling or kangaroo hopping (come here, no go away stuff) can occur throughout your day. Or you may even pull what feels like an 'emotional hamstring' without careful warm-up preparation, which may immobilise you and put you out of the game of life for a season or more. When some people are emotionally wounded and have no support, they give up the game of love and life altogether. These serious emotional wounds can be avoided with preparation, as we will see below.

Extra mile checkpoints

Before you commence your day it is important to be prepared. The difference between elite athletes and everyone else is that they 'go the extra mile' consistently. If you are aspiring to reach elite emotional fitness levels it is a must to go the extra mile by choosing to use the principles of emotional fitness every day. I have therefore created 'extra mile checkpoints', which will be useful if reviewed regularly to help you stay on track emotionally and gradually attain an elite level of emotional fitness.

Checkpoint 1 – Comfortable surroundings

If you are planning to speak to a particular person using an emotional fitness technique, choosing a comfortable environment is a key factor. Just as most people wear comfortable fitting clothes and shoes while doing physical workouts, the same principle applies to your emotional workout. Being emotionally comfortable is an essential ingredient for success. For example, being at work, in a public place or within earshot of others is not the optimum environment to do an emotional workout. Go to a park, sit in a car, get out of earshot of the kids or housemates and find a private place where you feel comfortable.

Checkpoint 2 – Uncomfortable surroundings

More often than not we don't get to plan when we need to use an emotional fitness technique. Life throws unexpected situations at us daily. While at work or in a meeting, shopping centre or restaurant, it is generally easier not to do a workout and let it pass. Most people either bite their tongue or unleash a verbal tirade. Emotional fitness is about responding with dignity – assertion not aggression. If you are unable to do this spontaneously, remove yourself and go back and address the situation when you can as I did at the lingerie shop. Don't pretend it never happened; address it when you are calmer.

Checkpoint 3 – Allocate adequate time

If you are choosing to speak to a specific person and do a workout, give yourself time and check that they have time. If they catch you on the spur of the moment with a difficult request or comment and you know you need to respond but there is not enough time, ask if you can get back to them when you and they have time. Dropping in on people or just phoning and commencing your workout with others does not lead to optimum results. It is suggested that you call first or write a letter or email and ask for a time that suits them.

If you wish to speak to your partner, sibling, parent or child, ask them to let you know when they can give you some time to chat to them rather than assuming that they will be receptive at any given moment. It helps to let them finish watching their favourite TV program, reading the chapter of a book, cooking the dinner or playing a computer game. You will then have their full attention and they won't feel that you have demanded their attention, but asked for it. People generally respond better when they feel they have been given a choice.

Checkpoint 4 – No emotional investment in the outcome

As I have previously mentioned, not everyone chooses to work on their emotional wellbeing. It is their right not to, and that needs to be respected. Whenever you practise an emotional fitness technique involving another person, it is imperative for your emotional health that you accept that they may not respond as you would hope. If you cannot do a particular workout without an emotional investment in the outcome, you are not ready to do it. You must be prepared for rejection, hostility, tears, anger or denial. How they respond is their business. How you conduct yourself is your focus while completing any emotional fitness workout.

Checkpoint 5 – Check your superiority/inferiority level

If you believe you are inferior or superior to another person you are in ego mode and dishonouring yourself and them. They may be a tulip and you a rose. You may much prefer roses – that is your choice – but a tulip is not better or worse than a rose, just different. If you cannot approach the other party with the understanding that you have different views from them, not superior or inferior, you are not ready to do a workout.

Checkpoint 6 – Are you expecting them to change?

If you are completing these exercises in the hope that the other person will change, your motive is about control – we need to control when we are afraid or stuck in shark mode and listening to repetitive fear tapes. If you think you have control issues, it is a good idea to spend time speaking with your personal trainer or dolphin before you begin a workout.

Checkpoint 7 – How do you get ready if you're not ready, but want to be?

Breathe, take your time and don't rush yourself. If you are unsure, that is a clear message that it is not time to do the workout yet. If you are not ready, don't do it – consult your emotional personal trainer (psychologist/counsellor/etc.) or your dolphin person, run the workout past them and ask for feedback. You may need to sleep on it. If you are ready but feeling a little anxious, remember to close your eyes and take slow breaths in and out – at least ten before you start.

Checkpoint 8 – Handling abuse

If the person becomes abusive during a workout, be prepared to remove yourself. If you feel yourself wanting to become physically abusive, or hear yourself being verbally abusive, remove yourself.

Checkpoint 9 – Interruptions and listening

Be prepared not to interrupt the other person while they are speaking. Listen to what they are saying and wait until they have finished. If you are unsure if they have finished, ask them before you start to respond. If they interrupt you, ask that you be heard; if they don't respect that, advise them that you will cease the conversation until they can be rational and let you have your say.

Checkpoint 10 – Shoulds and finger pointing

Try to erase the word 'should' from your dialogue. Should is about shame and expectation. Expectations that have not been met need to be discussed – people make mistakes. Preferences are gentler on relationships. Saying to another 'I would have preferred' rather than 'you should have' decreases shame in disagreements. Finger pointing is also about shame and is antagonistic. Remember, these exercises are about your emotional workout, not theirs.

Checkpoint 11 – People-pleasing is selfish, self-honouring is respectful

People-pleasing, or giving people their way, is a form of manipulation and is dishonest. It is about doing what they want so that they will like or love you more – it is an attempt to control another. Self-honouring, or speaking your truth responsibly, is about respecting their right to disagree with you and giving them credit for being adult enough to cope with it. If they do not cope with your speaking up or disagreeing, that is their right, and your right is to be who you are. Elite levels of emotional fitness are reached in relationships when both parties can agree to disagree in harmony without personalising. It is about principle not personality.

Emotional warm-up checkpoint

It's a good idea to warm up or emotionally stretch before your day begins – like checking a map before starting a journey. I do my warm-up exercise in bed each morning and am limbered up before I put my feet on the floor – with two teenage sons I can be given a workout three seconds after I open the bedroom door!

Check in with your four-year-old – your primary expert

Place a photograph of yourself in early childhood where you can see it daily. For optimum results, make eye contact with that wonderful child that is you before you embark on each and every day. Visualise taking him or her by the hand and assuring them that no matter what happens today you won't abandon them, or let anyone hurt or disrespect them. Emotional fitness is very much about parenting yourself in a constructive, dolphin-like manner. You must become your ideal parent to yourself. Gandhi put this beautifully when he said: 'We must become the change we wish to see in the world.'

If you don't have a photo, bring up a memory of a time when you were young, perhaps playing in your cubby, with the dog or at the beach. That child is still with you. The quality of your relationship with your child self dictates the quality of primary or intimate relationships in your life. Primary relationships involve vulnerability, so being considerate of your own vulnerability rather than frustrated by it, accelerates the level of your emotional fitness.

I use my morning visualisation of little Cynthia throughout the day. If I am about to do a daunting interview, a keynote address or a live television slot, I usually take myself to the ladies room, close the door, close my eyes and bring that picture into the forefront of my mind's eye. This vision calms and emotionally centres me and helps me remember to be true to myself by honouring that little girl that is me. In being connected to that pure part of myself, where my dolphin lives, I feel empowered and safe.

It is also imperative to remember to warm down at the end of your day. As an athlete needs to calm their body after a burst of peak performance, the emotions also need to settle after a day of high energy output.

Emotional warm-down checkpoints

I write about my day every evening – sometimes it's only a few words, other times it's a lot more. It helps me check in with me. I see my personal trainer less these days as I am now becoming my own personal trainer through these actions of self-parenting. I also don't need to speak with my dolphin person, Barbara, as much as I did in the early years. We tend to have big catch-ups every few months and just spend hours chatting. However, if a complex emotional issue comes up, I call my personal trainer or dolphin and verbalise my situation and what my thoughts are on how to handle it. They either validate me or offer alternative suggestions.

Here are the four warm-down checkpoints that I recommend.

Checkpoint 1 – Debrief with your emotional personal trainer or dolphin

Speaking about your day helps you unwind. Your personal trainer or dolphin is that chosen person in your life who believes in you and promotes your desire to become emotionally fitter. Recalling the events, the pleasing moments, the upsetting or confusing dialogue and the result with this person is essential for growth. If you have emotionally bruised yourself or another, or have forgotten a point on the extra mile checklist, you know you won't be shamed by this person, but motivated to improve. Mistakes are seen as valuable information, and debriefing with your trainer or dolphin will help you remember that.

Checkpoint 2 – Write about your workouts

Sometimes speaking to your personal trainer or dolphin daily will not be possible so I suggest that you buy yourself a blank book and record your progress (as a guide, see the the sample 'Personal progress' sheet on page 248) and use it to keep track of your growth. As elite athletes keep track of times, personal bests and ways to improve, this personal record will also help you to monitor your growth. If you have forgotten a point in the extra mile checkpoints, making a note of it will help you to remember next time. You can also revise your last workout and focus on areas in need of improvement. It is wonderful in years to come to look back and see proof in black and white of how much you have grown. It is also a valuable tool to use in debriefing and warm-up sessions with your personal trainer or dolphin.

Checkpoint 3 – Check in with your four-year-old – your primary expert

Look at the photo or bring up the visual memory of yourself as a child. Consider how that child coped throughout the day. Did you parent yourself well, or would you like to make changes for tomorrow? Under the heading 'How I parented myself' on the personal progress page, you are given the opportunity to review your emotional responses.

Checkpoint 4 – Relax and reward yourself

No matter what the outcome, you tried. Even if you forgot all the extra mile checkpoints, you still had a go at emotional fitness during your day and that took courage. Like running a marathon, it doesn't matter where you come in the race, or even if you finish, having a go is something to feel good about. Reward yourself with a treat – something you love to do or have. It may be an evening swim, a massage, some fresh seafood or a flower. You could even just put a gold star next to your entry on the relevant record page with a big tick for well done.

Notes from Tim Sharp

As you're probably starting to realise, emotional fitness, just like physical fitness, requires hard and regular work (or exercise). No successful athlete achieves any real success without hard work and frequent sessions involving 'blood, sweat and tears'. Although 'natural talent' helps some, even those with the best genetic make-up need to train and exercise their gifts in order to maximise their performance.

Just like a sportsperson, if you want to be an emotional athlete you'll need to begin to train hard and train often. Just like a sportsperson, you'll get out what you put in.

In the preceding chapters, Cynthia outlined some of the strategies that have helped her. You, too, might find these strategies helpful or you might even come up with different strategies with which you feel more comfortable. In my experience, the exact nature of the coping strategy is usually not as important as the effort a person puts into utilising any strategy and the focus they place on doing something (one could almost argue, anything) constructive.

For example, in the notes accompanying Chapter 2, I outlined some strategies derived from cognitive therapy. In simple terms, I advocated a staged process beginning with (1) learning how to be more aware of your thoughts and feelings, (2) not just accepting your thoughts and feelings but beginning to challenge and question them, and (3) working towards replacing unhelpful and self-defeating thoughts, feelings and behaviours with more helpful and constructive ones.

Most people trying this approach for the first time find it much more difficult than it sounds. At the same time, however, I always emphasise that achieving change is very possible and that if you view the application of these skills as simply that, the application of a 'skill', then you can apply yourself in the same way you've probably applied yourself to learning other new skills and again, in the same way, utilisation of skills tends to improve with practice and perseverance.

The major challenge at this stage of your emotional fitness training, therefore, is to begin to develop a system of strategies that you can begin to practise. Notice that I did not write that you'll begin to master or perfect them. I wrote that you'll begin to practise, because it's important that you have realistic expectations of yourself. The reality is, it will probably take you several weeks (at the least), or several months, or even several years to really master what Cynthia describes. But how long it takes does not, in my opinion, matter as much as how much effort you put in and whether you make at least some progress in the right direction.

Let's look at some specific examples advocated by Cynthia.

To begin with, she describes a morning warm-up. This is a great idea and one I frequently, if not always, recommend to my clients. If you start the day on a positive note then you significantly increase your chances of experiencing more positives throughout the day. On the other hand, if your first experiences are negative then everything that comes after can easily seem negative.

Second, focus on what you can change (i.e. you) and not on what you can't change (i.e. others). There's a great saying that goes something like 'Give me the strength to change what I can change, accept what I cannot change, and the wisdom to know the difference.'

While making efforts to change, however, recognise that we all make mistakes. This is okay, as long as you correct them as soon as possible. Although this reality is important to recognise, we obviously don't want to make mistakes if we can help it so try to ensure that, whenever possible, you set yourself up for success and not for failure. That is, use what Cynthia calls 'checkpoints' to ensure that you give yourself the best possible chance of achieving what you want to achieve. This might involve choosing your time and/or your surroundings to talk to someone. It might also involve practising what you're going to say and/or visualising yourself and your preferred outcome as positively as possible.

Third, at the end of a difficult encounter, or at the end of a difficult day, don't forget to warm down, just as an athlete would after a workout. Among other things, this will help you learn from your mistakes and reward yourself for your successes. Both of these – reward and reprimand – are very important activities. Give yourself a pat on the back (or something more substantial if you want to) when you've done something good or responded in a positive way.

Just as important, however, is to be responsible for your mistakes. If you've made a mistake, or done something that you are not proud of, differentiate between your behaviour and you. For example, instead of telling yourself 'I'm bad for doing …' try 'I would prefer not to repeat that behaviour, but I am still proud of myself for trying to make things better. Next time I would prefer to handle it this way …' and write about how you would like to respond next time a situation like this arises.

And finally, as Cynthia and I have both emphasised already, don't think you have to do all this on your own. Utilise whatever support you have available to you. This might be a professional 'trainer' (such as a psychologist) or a mentor (such as Cynthia's friend) or it might even be a family member in whom you have the utmost trust and respect. In addition, it is advisable to utilise other available resources such as your diary, self-help books (of which there are many good ones) and even the Internet. And check the 'Contacts' section at the back of this book.

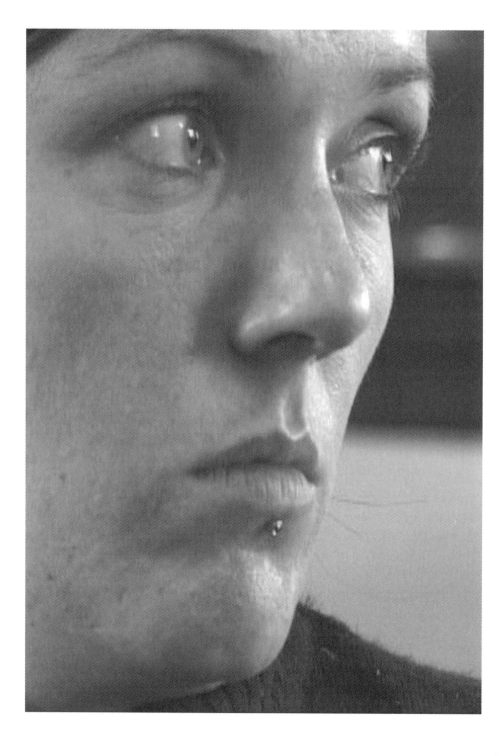

5 Your emotional history

I was wedged between the wardrobe and the wall, holding onto my knees in an attempt to comfort myself. I wanted to feel held but did not want human touch. Anyone who tried to touch me in a caring way seemed to cause me emotional pain. It was like disinfectant on a wound. It hurt. The pale blue hospital gown that was tied up at the back was pulled over my knees. I had been staring at its linen pattern that was soaked in my tears and snot for hours as if it was the only thing that existed in the world.

My mind was blank. There was nothing left inside me, not even tears and definitely not words. I felt like a dry and barren desert consumed by an eerie silence. I was alone – my friend, the never empty champagne glass, coupled with the nutty taste of tobacco in a big, fat joint, had left me for someone else. I was no fun to party with any more. All of my laughter had drained away.

Barbara, my dolphin, had found me naked the day before in foetal position, lying in the bath with the shower water beating down on me. I had been there for hours. I was mute and shaking, remembering the horrors of my childhood. I had post-traumatic stress. I felt insane. I had been sixteen months clean and sober and I was coming undone.

I was in a psychiatric hospital, again. I had been in a place like this before at age sixteen after my first suicide attempt. I remember being so angry then, when I awoke in intensive care, because I was still alive.

But now I was 34 – separated from my husband, scaring the crap out of my old circle of party friends, who had all seemed to have just vanished, and out of contact with my biological family since I had started to set new boundaries. My father was dead. I was pleased about that, as I would have been too scared to speak about his abuse had he been alive. When he was alive, even though I was 26 and a grown woman, I would duck every time he raised his hand to scratch his head for fear of being hit.

Barbara had brought in a bunch of yellow roses. I was so angry with her. She was being so nice to me. What was her problem? And then there was Brad, the guy I was now living with. He would come to visit me and sit next to me with tears of love in his eyes. God, what a loser – he must be desperate to want someone like me!

There was a knock at the door. It broke my staring trance. I unwedged myself from the wardrobe's embrace, wiped my nose and quickly got back into bed. The shrink entered.

'Hi, my name is Mal, how are you feeling?' he asked in a gentle but professional way.

'Just great,' I replied sarcastically, challenging him as I gave him a bitchy smile. 'I'm in a loony bin, I could easily lose custody of my two kids being in here, I am going insane, but I'm clean and sober and look where it's got me. Yep, life's just great!'

He was dressed in shorts that needed an iron and a polo shirt with the collar not turned down properly. His hair, curly and unruly, gave him a relaxed look. I liked him; he looked like a family man. There was no way I was going to let him know I approved of him though.

'I was abused by my dad and the man next door, we were beaten as kids and so was my mother. Dad was an alcoholic, Mum has a serious drinking problem, and my sister uses religion like I used drugs and alcohol and is convinced that I'm just possessed by the devil and if I don't wear earrings and my kids stop watching *The Simpsons* I will be just fine. I can't have sex because I have anxiety fits and flashbacks to all the hideous childhood stuff, and these flashbacks are starting to happen while I'm doing the food shopping. I am living with a guy who is trying to love me and I feel like I am wrapped in barbed wire and any time he tries to touch me it hurts me and him. I am paranoid about my weight and my hair and obsess about not being good enough. My kids don't know what's wrong with me and I feel insane, so the question is can you fix me?' I demanded without drawing a breath, believing that he would put me in the too hard basket and assign me to someone else.

'You are not insane; you have chronic Post-Traumatic Stress Disorder because of your history. You are no different from a Vietnam Vet who has seen too much trauma and who, after returning from war, runs for a bunker any time he hears a news helicopter in the sky. It is like you have undetonated land mines in your mind. We need to disarm them. It will take time. I don't think you need medication, but I do think you need to get back to your kids and get back into your life. You don't need to be in here – it is doing you more harm than good. I will need to see you at least once a week. You need to give this process at least five to seven years, but it can be done,' he said calmly and respectfully.

'Five years!' I spat at him. 'I will be an old woman, I'll be nearly 40.'

'Well, your alternative is to continue living like this. It's up to you and how committed you are,' he answered matter of factly.

I am now almost 41. I have been working with my personal trainer, Mal, for six years and my dolphin, Barbara, for eight years. I have not had any PTSD episodes for two years.

My emotional history was tripping me up because I did not know how to deal with it. Now I do, and the exercises in this book are what helped me do it.

Are you carrying any emotional injuries?

Prior to commencing a physical workout regime it is advisable to have a checkup with your GP to check your heart rate and blood pressure and to address any old physical war wounds you may have – old football injuries, back problems, irregular heart rhythm and so on. Any professional health club will request a full physical history before they will allow you to use their facilities. This is so that people with specific injuries don't do exercises that will damage them further. It is also to help the personal trainer who is preparing your personal workout to help you attain your optimum level of physical fitness.

Again, the same principle applies to emotional fitness workouts. If you have a serious emotional wounding, such as I had, you will have to go slower than someone who does not.

Why are some people unable to just forget and move on?

Those who don't understand emotional wounding are often heard to say, 'Oh, for God's sake, it happened 30 years ago, just get over it!' And they become frustrated at the individual who cannot keep up with them emotionally. Let's describe why with this scenario.

Imagine two athletes training separately for a triathlon. One falls over during a training session and grazes his knee badly. It is a surface wound. It hurts and immobilises him for a little while, but it heals and, in time, the scar disappears. The second athlete falls over while training, but down an embankment, and his upper thigh is impaled on a rusty fence post. He does a great deal of muscle damage and is hospitalised. This is physical trauma, not a surface wound. It will take longer to heal and there will always be a scar.

Now if the first athlete with the surface wound rings the second athlete with the deep wound and says, 'Come on, mate, I had an accident as well, but it has healed. Don't be such a baby, just get over it, the triathlon is this Sunday', I would hope that once the first athlete had been informed of the severity of the wound he would have some compassion and understanding as to why his mate could not keep up with him physically for a while.

Emotional wounding works the same way, but it is invisible. The people who are often heard saying 'Oh, for God's sake, just get over it' are in one of two places themselves. They are either totally uninformed and genuinely don't understand the difference between a surface emotional wound and severe emotional trauma or, more often than not, they have never experienced an emotional trauma so have no under-standing of how immobilising it can be and the time involved in its healing. This is why we cannot always 'keep up' emotionally with others who have not experienced such wounding.

The other reason for such a dismissive response is that the person is living in denial of their own emotional trauma, and has learnt how to sufficiently suppress it with some form of emotional escapism, such as exercise, work, drugs, alcohol or food. Such people become quickly annoyed by anyone who is looking at their issues and often try to shame the other into submission.

What is the difference between a surface emotional wound and deep emotional trauma?

Everybody experiences emotional bruises and grazes throughout life. Again, the level of vulnerability involved in the relationship is what makes the difference in the depth of the wound. For example, if somebody dies in your tertiary circle, it is less devastating than if someone passes away in your primary circle. The death of a distant uncle you see every now and then will be less traumatic than the death of your mother or father.

Some examples of emotional bruises and grazes are:

- being called names
- being yelled at abusively in traffic
- not being invited to a party
- being dumped by a first love at school
- being ignored.

Of course, the intensity of the emotional surface wound increases with the level of vulnerability in the relationship. These issues are easier to handle when they occur with tertiary people than if they happen with a secondary or primary person.

Some examples of deep emotional trauma are:

- death of a loved one (no counselling or support)
- killing another (war, accidents)
- witnessing a tragedy (September 11, terrorism, bushfires, droughts, crimes)
- rape and other acts of violence (domestic violence, torture of animals)
- childhood abuse (sexual/physical)
- abandonment (unresolved adoption issues, childhood death of a parent or sibling, emotional neglect, constant criticism and belittlement of a child).

Why are some people so emotionally sensitive?

People who carry unresolved deep emotional trauma or injury are no different from a person nursing an undressed physical wound. If a person has a broken limb that has not been plastered the slightest touch of that limb will result in excruciating pain for them. Until the arm is supported that person is hypersensitive. The same applies for those with unresolved emotional trauma. Until they get the correct support the slightest touch can hurt them deeply. These people are often described as overreacting, whereas often it is underlying emotional wounding that is causing the hypersensitivity.

What can you do if you are carrying emotional injuries?

If you have recently been emotionally bruised with a surface wound it is advisable to be gentle with yourself and definitely not attempt primary/advanced workouts.

If you carry any deep emotional trauma, it is not advisable to commence this work without a personal trainer or reliable dolphin; both are advised for optimum results. It is also important not to compare your progress with that of others.

If you are still emotionally medicating on drugs or alcohol it is not advisable to attempt any of these workouts before you are clean or sober. Aspiring to be emotionally fit while emotionally numbed on drugs and/or alcohol is a bit like eating ice cream and fried chicken on a tread-mill – you are sabotaging your attempt at a healthier life and setting yourself up for failure.

Notes from Tim Sharp

In this chapter Cynthia sets the scene for those of you considering commencing an emotional fitness program. In doing so, she makes a number of crucial points. Each of these points deserves serious consideration prior to beginning your fitness program.

To begin with, it is important to examine the extent to which you have been 'injured' in the past and, accordingly, the extent to which you might have existing or old injuries (or 'war wounds'). Just as most gyms and personal trainers conduct a physical assessment, including measures of blood pressure, height and weight, etc., before starting you on a physical program, it is advisable that you conduct your own emotional assessment prior to commencing your emotional fitness program. Alternatively, if you think it would be helpful, or necessary, you could also consider seeking a professional opinion.

As noted by Cynthia, a full assessment of old injuries is important as it will partly determine the level at which you can and should engage in emotional fitness training. To some degree, it will also determine the extent to which you can and will benefit from the emotional fitness program on your own (or the extent to which you might consider seeking professional assistance).

At the same time, however, and as emphasised by Cynthia, even the most serious and long-standing wounds can heal, given time and effort. Some readers might associate completely with Cynthia's examples and her past. Others might read her story and feel that although they relate to her distress there are significant differences in the nature of events that occurred.

Mostly, it doesn't really matter. If you're distressed about things that have occurred in your life and if, as a result, you believe that you are not as emotionally fit as you would like to be, then regardless of what has happened or of what is happening in your life now you can, as Cynthia so admirably proves, learn how to train so that you can improve your emotional fitness and, with dedication and time, become fitter, stronger and more flexible than you have previously been.

Along the way, another important issue to which we suggest you give serious consideration is the time and effort you will need to devote to your fitness regime. Remember, no Olympic athlete achieved his or her successes easily. Even local sportsmen and -women have to train to achieve the level of performance and skill they need to participate in whatever competition they are participating in. To use a popular cliché, you will get out of your training what you put in.

Now, if you're thinking that it sounds like too much hard work, ask yourself, as Cynthia asked herself when confronted by the prospect of five years or so of therapy, what are the alternatives? Is it any 'easier' to continue living life the way you are at present? Is it ever really 'too late' to change? Surely enjoying five, ten, twenty years of improved emotional fitness is better than none at all. Remember, you can't change the past but you can create your future.

At the same time, however, don't ever compare your progress with others. Just because one person achieved certain things over a certain amount of time does not mean it will necessarily take you as long, or that you must achieve the same in the same time frame. Everyone is different and everyone commences training with a different history and with different 'wounds'. Some will find it easier than others. Some will progress faster than others.

As long as you're doing what you need to do and as long as you remind yourself that help is available and you don't have to do it all on your own (especially if your wounds are long-term and deep) then you will move forward at your own pace and you will eventually achieve what you want to achieve (which may not be the same thing someone else wants to achieve!).

6

How to use the workouts

W e were sitting in peak hour traffic and we were running a little late. I didn't mind because it meant I had more time to spend with my beautiful Barb.

I just love everything about her. Her smell, the skin on her eyelids, how soft it is and the way it gently moves when she smiles. I actually use her hands in my morning warm-ups. I visualise them as a comforting image and imagine my little four-year-old as a tiny fairy sitting in her palm being maternally cradled from the harshness of daily life.

She was chatting away as she always does. I was not really listening to her words but the melodic tone of her voice. Time with her is so precious it feels like emotional cash – like someone has given me millions of dollars that I can put in the bank for later. I always feel in credit after spending time with Barb.

'Oh come on then, possum, in you come', she gently said, lifting her elegant hand from the steering wheel to give the other driver a signal that she would let them in.

The car in front of us had not indicated. It was pushing its way into our lane. I knew it was highly likely that if I had been driving I would have yelled an obscenity at the driver. I smiled to myself and thought, 'God, I want to be like that.'

The emotional fitness workouts

I wrote the workouts in the following chapter around three years ago to help me with emotional issues I found hard to handle. I typed them and then bound them in a book. Each morning, after my warm-up, I randomly flick through my book and open at a page. The page I open at always seems to be the appropriate message for me on that day. How you use these workouts is up to you. You may choose to work through them one by one, or just select those you feel are relevant to your emotional life at the moment, or take the random flick approach.

These workouts are currently being used in the corporate sector, by parents, teachers and students, in hospitals, gaols and schools, and as discussion topics at a range of different recovery services. And I still use them every day.

The way it works for me is that, as I wake each morning, I feed myself the emotional vitamins I need, which are just as necessary as breakfast and a shower. My kneejerk reaction without these workouts would be to go into shark thoughts as soon as I opened my eyes. I short-circuit my shark tapes, or eject them if you like, by starting the day with a dolphin message in the form of a workout. I read the workout aloud to myself so that the vibration of my own voice actually activates my dolphin. In this way I am actually emotionally ingesting positive dolphin tapes to help build my personal library. And as a result of doing this over the years I have become fitter and healthier, not just emotionally but overall.

The 'Personal Progress' page

This is part of your warm-down routine, as mentioned previously, and I recommend that it be done after every workout. It helps you and your personal trainer and/or dolphin monitor your progress. Having kept a personal record of my emotional fitness over a number of years, I find it interesting to go back and look at what I found almost insurmountable in the early days. It gives me a sense of accomplishment and helps me remember that there are no hurdles that cannot be overcome.

An example of a Personal Progress page is given on page 248.

Emotional fitness goals

As people have goals they strive to reach in their levels of physical fitness, people also have goals they would like to attain in emotional fitness. It is a good idea to list the goals you would like to achieve that you are currently finding difficult. For example:

- working out what love and intimacy is for you
- overcoming chronic people-pleasing
- understanding why you worry so much
- accepting that a relationship has come to an end.

It helps a great deal to write down the areas of emotional fitness you would like to work on so that you can give special attention to the specific workouts that help with these areas.

Some tips before you start

I started all of my workouts at the beginner's level and went slowly to build up my confidence. Then I moved onto intermediate, where the emotional output was more demanding. These days, I do the advanced workouts whenever life challenges me.

The advanced level is still a solid workout for me, as I believe it will be for you too, because the fitter you become emotionally the more you will able to take on – as with physical fitness. When you first commence training it's about building strength and with strength comes endurance. It is not recommended that people commencing physical exercise for the first time try to complete a triathlon on their first weekend. But eventually they will be able to if they don't give up.

You will be able to complete emotional triathlons in life and reach elite levels of emotional fitness if you commit to these workouts – it's a promise.

Speaking of emotional triathlons, writing this book has been one for me. It has been far more challenging than my first book because I am sharing intimate real life experiences that I did not have the emotional capacity to do three years ago. Some of my stories have actually been an advanced workout to write. My heart pounded and tears rolled down my cheeks, but I knew that on the other side of the fear would be empowerment.

When you begin to use the emotional fitness workouts, I would advise that you go gently and start as a beginner with tertiary people, as you would if you were starting yoga, kick boxing or any form of physical exercise you had never tried before. You may find that you are emotionally fitter than you thought, and the beginner workouts may be a breeze for you. If this is the case, move onto the intermediate/secondary workouts and then onto the advanced/primary level when you feel that you are ready.

As with physical fitness, repetition is the key. Building emotional strength takes time and is a process, not a quick solution. I recommend repeating the same workout for a few weeks until you find it is easy and then progress to the next level.

It is dangerous for your emotional health to rush and begin these workouts at an advanced level, just as it would be unsafe to pick up a heavy weight far beyond your physical capacity during your first week of training. You could hurt yourself and perhaps even do some serious damage.

Please take your time – you don't want to burn yourself out.

7 30 Emotional workouts

1. Keeping up appearances

2. Common senses

3. Reality overload

4. Receiving respect

5. Running away from self

6. Smother mothers

7. Following intuition

8. An emotional Bandaid called denial

9. Emotionally medicating

10. Asking for help – the beginning of the end

11. Letting go

12. Oh, to just feel good enough

13. Grieving for the perfect family fairytale

14. What is love?

15. Coping with remorse

16. Personal boundaries

17. Being vulnerable

18. Responsible anger

19. Hope or expectation?

20. Safe friendships

21. Dealing with the ex-partner

22. Beautiful sexual intimacy

23. Giving and receiving affection

24. Understanding emotionally unavailable people

25. Conserving emotional fuel

26. Freedom from worrying about what others think

27. Deserving success, money and recognition

28. Trusting in trust

29. Controlling my need to control

30. Accepting acceptance

1. Keeping up appearances

*Half the time I'm so exhausted I don't know whether I'm
coming or going. It's like I'm on this nonstop merry-go-round
and I can't get off. Antonio pushes himself just as hard or
harder than me, and I want to keep up.*

Melanie Griffith

I grew up in what I call Ken and Barbie land because everything visible
to the eye looked pretty and perfect.

My mother in the early Sixties was a knockout. She would wear
purple miniskirts, long black 'come and get me' boots with one of those
bouffant hairstyles that was so full of hairspray it did not move on a
windy day. Her black cat eyeliner and cleavage were always present
before we left the house.

I remember being perhaps four years of age and travelling on a bus
into the city of Adelaide with her. An old lady sitting opposite was
smiling at us.

'Is she your little sister, love, she looks a lot like you?' the old woman
asked my mother.

'No, no, this is my youngest daughter, Cindy. Her older sister is at
school', Mum said with delight.

I was always called Cindy even though I was named Cynthia at birth.
Dad had invited a business colleague over for dinner one night when
Mum was pregnant with me and all he did was speak with great pride
about his beautiful wife, Cynthia. Mum decided there and then that I
would not be called Gaynor, but Cynthia; I suppose she hoped that one
day a man would speak about me in that way. But when I was born she
said I did not look like a Cynthia, but a Cindy, and she could never bring
herself to use my full name. Even now, she does not like to use it.

'Oh my goodness, your figure is far too slim, you look like a model,
not a mother', the old woman said with sincerity.

'Aren't you a lucky girl to have such a beautiful mother?' the woman
said to me waiting for a response.

I just looked out the window and thought to myself, 'No, I wish I had a mother who smelled like baked bread, wore an apron and looked like that mother on the TV program, "The Waltons".'

My father was the Ken doll, and his name was Ken – no kidding. He was a GI Joe type of bloke, a craggily handsome Charles Bronson-looking man. He was perhaps 178 centimetres tall, with dark hair and olive skin, and a real ladies' man. I remember many times my mother being in tears because he had made passes at her friends, or she had found another woman's earrings in his pockets. He was a womaniser and a very charismatic flirt.

And guess where we lived? Well where else would Ken and Barbie live but in a suburb called Paradise in Adelaide, South Australia.

My mother worked so hard at being perfect. She had one of those beautiful Barbara Streisand noses. I thought her face and skin were divine. But I remember her coming home from the hospital one day with black eyes and a plaster over her nose. I was so sad for her. She said that Dad used to say her face was perfect except for her nose. I loved her nose. So her nose was changed and it always confused me because I thought it made her special the way it was.

She also lived on Ford diet pills. I remember the yellow cylindrical containers they came in, with red lids. I used to keep my Barbie dolls' shoes in them when they were empty.

So our house was always tidy – fresh flowers on the table and clean linen on our beds. But the violence seemed to make our house feel chaotic. The yelling and screaming, the tears and slammed doors, made it a place I longed to escape from.

The physical and the material were priorities in our home. No-one knew what to do with the emotional other than deny or suppress it. If we cried the response was 'Stop your crying or I'll give you something to cry about' and if we laughed too much it was 'Settle down and stop being so silly.'

Emotion was not acceptable. I learnt that at a very young age. And so I grew into an adult who only knew how to relate to others on physical and material levels. If I wanted to emotionally interact I needed a substance to help me, as my parents did.

My first marriage mimicked my childhood home. I found my Ken doll at age nineteen. However, in all my wisdom at this young age, I thought I was being very clever in my choice. The man I chose was physically not at all like my father. My father was short, dark, uneducated, from a low economic background and a violent alcoholic. I chose for a husband a tall, blonde, university educated man from an affluent background, and a mellow drug user. Because I lived in the physical and material realms I thought that someone physically opposite to my father would result in a marriage with opposite results. My parents had divorced in my early teens. I was looking for the happy ever after ending.

We did not date, I stalked him. I was a predatory female. I could not handle men who showed interest in me first – I needed control – plus if men wanted me I thought they must be desperate. This guy was not assertive; I hunted him down, climbed into his bedroom window at night and attached myself to him. He did not resist.

Our married life lasted nine years, but we lived together for about thirteen years.

I lived on diet pills, starved myself and had cosmetic surgery. The house was perfect and I became a plastic Barbie. I measured my self-worth on the bathroom scales every morning. We were violent and only connected with the help of drugs and alcohol.

He remains a fit and handsome man. I tried so desperately to keep up with him, to be good enough, slim enough, sexy enough and intelligent enough. My childhood life was all about how it looked to the outside world. Keeping up appearances was my carbon copy of how people must live, and I acted it out in my adult life. I was so exhausted most of the time; I wanted to keep up with my husband and what a perfect and normal wife would be like. It was like a nonstop merry-go-round. I am so glad I got off.

◎ Workout 1

Keeping up appearances

I will today let go of society's yardstick of what is normal. Keeping up appearances is about me abandoning my truth so that I can align myself with some imaginary expectation that I believe I must live up to.

I will remember today that there are no normal people. 'Normal' is a cycle on my washing machine, and not much else. Everybody has emotional stuff they are dealing with, no matter who they are and how they appear. Most people spend the second half of their lives getting over the first. That saying 'The only normal people you know are the people you don't know very well' is true. Everybody has flaws and insecurities on some level and makes mistakes.

The need to keep up appearances is an indicator that I am emotionally unfit in this area, for it entails deceiving myself or another. If I have to lie or pretend to gain the acceptance of another, I am telling myself that my truth is unacceptable, and therefore I am unacceptable.

I would not ask a four-year-old child to pretend for approval, so why ask myself today?

I enjoy the company of others who flaunt their flaws, don't take themselves too seriously and can have a laugh about life. I find relief in that sort of company. I choose to be that sort of company for someone else today. I will be more honest about who I am and who I'm not. I choose to be a safe person for whom people don't have to keep up appearances.

I will focus on keeping up with myself today, rather than keeping up appearances. These are some responses I may choose to use today:

◎ ◎ ◎ ◎ ◎

I have to be honest about this ... No, I'm not up to it today ... I like to be messy sometimes ... I don't have to work/exercise/diet/get dressed every day ... I can have a break ... I deserve a treat ... I just don't feel like it.

Now go to page 248, photocopy the 'Personal Progress' page there, add the appropriate workout number and name, and fill the page in.

2. Common senses

I keep hearing tree talk, water words, and I keep knowing
what they mean.
Lucille Clifton

I had a favourite spot in the backyard under a tree. It was my spot. Like the shape a mattress takes on after being slept on for years, this area of lawn in the backyard cradled my body every time I lay there – Mother Earth seemed to be holding me in her bare hands.

I was not yet school age, so probably around four years old, when I found this magical place that no-one else knew about. It was like an imaginary friend. I would spend time with it, and nobody knew what I was really doing. They could not see the magic – only I understood the secret treasures this area of earth held.

I always waited until after lunch. That was the perfect time. The sun was in just the right place and would draw me out into the backyard like a huge magnet in the sky. I rarely wore shoes around home and just loved the soft texture of the grassy earth kissing the soles of my feet as they were relieved of the cold, uncaring, hard tiled floor inside our house.

I would check that no-one was watching and then tiptoe over to my spot. The grass around the area I lay on had a special pattern. As I lowered my small body back onto the earth and then rested my little head I felt like I was an astronaut getting ready for take off. I would place my arms, palms down, either side of me as if my hands were connecting with Mother Earth's cool palms. I held onto her grassy fingers and felt like she was welcoming me home. I would close my eyes and take a deep breath. Sometimes tears rolled down my cheeks – I did not know why, but I liked the gentle tickle of the salty tears as they rolled into my ear. It gave me a feeling of gentle pleasure.

I would become aware of the heaviness in my body – the bruises and the throbbing heat that came from my pubic bone. I didn't like living inside this shell. I wished I was a sparrow, so I could fly away.

I could smell the rich chocolate earth and the clean air that the tree above me provided. I became aware of the lingering taste of my peanut butter sandwich that I had just washed down with a glass of milk. I could hear the almost silent actions of the little sparrows hopping around on the tree's arms above me. I would lie there for quite some time, allowing my senses to converse with Mother Nature. If I listened to her for long enough she took the throbbing pain away from me. She drained away all the confusion in my head and replaced it with a sense of peace – then I would open my eyes.

The translucent green leaves against the blue summer sky were so perfect that they looked like a postcard picture. I loved Mother Nature's silent language of colour. And then there were the cloud stories she told me. She would lift me up and place me inside the soft cotton wool shapes and let me walk around inside the cloud with her. I could feel the fairyfloss texture of the clouds beneath my feet. Sometimes I would sit on the soft edge of the cloud and dangle my feet in the air – so high above the world – and look down at the little girl's body lying so still in that backyard below me. I met friendly dragons and fluffy cloud rabbits, and I just loved cloud story time.

It would then be time to roll over onto my tummy and chat to the sparrows which had been patiently waiting for their turn with me. So like a little battery that needed to be charged up on both sides, I would slowly roll over and fold my arms under my chin to rest my head. I loved the mighty sparrows so much. I actually wrote this poem about them when I began to write my very first book 30 years later. It details my intimate relationship with them, which started way back then when I was such a little girl.

The Mighty Sparrows

My heroes, my lifesavers, my beautiful friends
So small but so mighty
Silent to the end

No words needed just gentle comfort and a smile
Always come to visit, but only stay a little while
Cannot hold you, cannot touch you
My heart knows you must be free

A busy bird, many souls need you
Not only me

Mousy feathers mirror the colour of my hair
Sort of silvery brown like a little church mouse
You saved my life and gave me hope
By coming to visit my house

Without your blinking eyes and twitching head
A vision that brought me peace
Without your friendliness and time
Belief in beauty and freedom for me would surely cease

A small soaring soul magnificent in its plainness
No-one to impress; many just pass you by
A wise and gentle messenger
You helped me believe I some day would fly

Can't do this book without you
Am I worthy of this plight?
Please stay with me dear sparrow
Help me believe in the deep, dark quiet of the night

We've come so far together
Don't know how much more to go
I look for you at the bread shop
I look for you everywhere I go

Thank you my darling sparrows
My life's heroes that always make me smile
Cheeky fat little tummies
You've made all the pain worthwhile.

The sparrows would stay and chat for a while, but they were busy birds
that had many jobs to do. I would watch them disappear into the blue of

the sky and wonder where they went at night. I wondered where they slept and what they did during thunderstorms. But I knew I need not worry about them. These birds walked on the backs of lions, rhinoceros and crocodiles; they knew how to take care of themselves.

The sun would kiss my skin with its soothing warmth – I often felt like a lizard recharging in the sun to gain energy and mobility. There was also a lovely vine that draped itself over the back fence. It had purple trumpet-like flowers. While lying on my tummy I made myself into a small fairy and would fly inside the hollow throat of the flower and let the delicious purple colour engulf me. Hours would pass before I would be ready to leave my special spot.

Time in the backyard grounded me. I lay on Mother Earth as a child whenever I felt afraid or overwhelmed.

I remember one night – I think it was Christmas or New Year's Eve. I had been babysat at the next-door neighbour's house. He was a very cruel pedophile. He had hurt me badly before he put me to bed. My little body was very sore. I was woken out of a deep sleep by the over-powering smell of alcohol.

'Come on, time to go, time to go, hold onto Dad', my father slurred. He must have already taken my sister home and left me for the last trip. As we walked through the dark house and out the front door I could hear music in the street – other neighbours were having parties.

'You can walk home from here, can't you? Dad's just going to visit Keith and have a drink with him; tell Mummy I won't be long. I'll come and tuck you in later', he said as he tapped me on the bottom.

My eyes filled up with tears as he disappeared inside a door further down the street. I was in a daze and upset. I knew that when he came back to tuck me in he would be drunker, and it was always the worst sort of tuck-in when he was drunk. My little body was already throbbing with pain.

It was a beautiful balmy summer's night. I lay myself down on the cool front lawn. My thin cotton pyjamas let the coolness of the night's earth comfort my skin. I lay there very still and looked up at the night sky. The stars were beautiful. Hot tears filled my eyes. I blinked and they rolled silently down my face. Mother Nature was smiling at me with her starry eyes. She knew everything that was happening; she loved me and calmed me with her presence. I became sleepy and curled up into a ball. She cuddled me with the soft earth. She would get me through the night, I knew it.

◎ Workout 2

Common senses

No matter where I am in the world today the sky and the earth are there for me. If I am imprisoned, Mother Nature can visit me through my memory – she is very resourceful.

My senses are what will help me make sense of my life today, if I remember to use them. I can use my senses to ground or centre myself and bring me back to the here and now – if I need to. Sight, smell, taste, touch and sound – my five senses – I choose to use them all today and be aware of the difference it makes.

I choose to consciously look for beauty today, in myself or another – perhaps go to an art gallery, get up to watch the sunrise or take time out to watch it set, or maybe watch the surf or a bird soaring in the sky. I could choose today to wear a colour that I love to bring me pleasure. I will look into the eyes of someone I love today and really see them.

◎ ◎ ◎ ◎ ◎

I could wear a fragrance or wash myself with a scented soap that I find pleasing. I could burn some incense or put a scented car freshener in my car. I could purchase some fragrant flowers today for my home or desk to arouse my sense of smell. I will gently press my nose into the nape of the neck of those I hug today and smell their being.

◎ ◎ ◎ ◎ ◎

I choose to taste what I eat today rather than just swallow it. I could ask my taste buds what they feel like eating rather than just purchasing food or cooking whatever is in the fridge.

◎ ◎ ◎ ◎ ◎

Today I could wear something with a texture that pleases me – maybe a silk tie, a soft cotton T-shirt, a velvet item or a fluffy woollen jumper. I will take time out to touch someone I love or care about flesh on flesh; for example, holding hands, placing my palm on their cheek.

◎ ◎ ◎ ◎ ◎

I could be more aware of sounds today. I could find time to listen to nature or beautiful music, or to become more aware of the sound of the voices of those I love.

◎ ◎ ◎ ◎ ◎

My five senses give me valuable information; I choose to be more aware of them today:
I will see, rather than just look … I can pay more attention to fragrances and aromas … I will choose my favourite tastes … I can focus more on touching as a form of communication … I can soothe my soul with beautiful music or words.

Now go to the back of the book, and photocopy and fill in the 'Personal Progress' page.

3. Reality overload

No-one ever finds life worth living; they have to make it
worth living.

Author unknown

He was a blonde god. Tanned and muscular, all the girls wanted him, and he knew it. His name was Harry and he made me nervous every time he looked at me. He was too good to be true for someone like me. I was sixteen, nearly seventeen, and had never had consenting sex. He was an older man, aged nineteen.

Harry knew I had never slept with anyone and hunted me like a wolf. He had piercing blue eyes and a strong square jaw. He was not affectionate or warm, but physically driven. He looked at me as though he wanted to devour me. I knew that energy and understood it; it was a predator's stare – I remembered it from childhood.

I had been going to nightclubs for quite some time – since I was fifteen actually. I was tall and looked older than I was. I loved to dance, I loved alcohol, I loved all the Eighties' disco music.

Harry would speak to other girls all night – they approached him. He and his long, blonde-haired surfer mates never moved from the bar. The women all came to them. Towards the end of the evening he would beckon me with a head movement to come over and speak to him. I would always wait for his nod and be so grateful when it happened. I was mesmerised, but afraid of him.

'Let's go', he would state, as he put his empty glass on the bar.

I would say nothing and just follow him, feeling lucky as all the other girls watched us leave. He could have said those words to any girl, but he chose me. He had been choosing me mostly for the past five months.

The night it all happened was like any other. He gave me the nod and we walked down the beach road to his white van. It was parked outside the surf club with the back facing the ocean. No doubt he had chosen this position so that he could just walk over the rocks and straight onto the beach at sunrise for a surf. He opened the back hatch of the van and left it open so that we would be able to see the ocean. It was probably around 2 a.m. – the stars in the sky were beautiful. We climbed in; there was silence as he took off his shirt. He rarely spoke to me.

Over the previous five months there had been heavy petting, but I would get really frightened and ask him to stop. We had never gone the whole way. He never complained – well he never said anything really; he would just get off me, open the van door and go outside for a while. He would then climb into the front of the van and drive me home while I lay half-dressed in the back. I was always sure I would never get the 'let's go' nod again from him, but months kept passing and he kept choosing me.

That night, he followed his normal seduction routine and we were almost at the point where I would gently plead with the sound of pending tears in my voice, 'No, no … please don't … I don't want to Harry, please stop, no more.' But this time he actually spoke. He looked into my eyes and said, 'Please don't say no, I will be gentle, I won't hurt you. You will really like it, I promise.'

He had never really looked into my eyes while we were in the back of his van or spoken much to me. My heart pounded. I wanted to please him. I wanted to be his girlfriend and maybe having sex with him would be what it would take. The moon was full and the light from the surf club glowed gently on his huge muscular frame. He was divine, he was a trophy.

'Okay.' I looked at him, I was terrified, I did not want to, but I was physically unable to say no. My body wanted him but my heart was on a warning alarm, trying to tell me it was dangerous. I did not listen.

Tears rolled down my cheeks as he removed my underpants. I remembered this feeling of being overpowered and afraid. He started to make deep guttural sounds; I had heard them before. His smell changed to a salty, musky scent. I went numb.

I don't recall the actual event, I emotionally blacked out. I left my body. It's what I used to do when I was a little girl – unplug my heart and leave my physical shell.

I awoke the next morning with the hot sun burning me through the van windows. He was out in the surf. He would be gone for hours. I felt disempowered and very, very sad.

Later that day as I sat on the beach I saw him walking along the water-front with another girl. I know he saw me, but he did not acknowledge me. He kept walking with a slim, tanned beauty in a string bikini. She was attempting to jump onto his back to have a piggyback ride. Eventually she was successful and hooked her long legs around his torso as he tucked the non-hamburger-eating hand behind his back and held onto her beautiful bottom.

I remember that I did not speak that day. I could not even cry. It was like I was emotionally frozen. I stayed like that for days. He never called or gave me the 'let's go' nod again.

My mother eventually took me to the local doctor and he prescribed some tranquillisers. I locked myself in a toilet block and took the whole bottle.

I remember looking into my own pupils just wanting to leave the pain and this thing called life. I felt dead inside. I did not know the person looking back at me – she was a stranger.

I had flashbacked to all of the degrading memories of sexual interactions between me and my father and the man next door when I was a child. Having sex with him put me into a state of reality overload. If this was sex, and that's what it meant to be a female, I wanted off this planet. It was a bad joke and I wanted no part of it. It had never really registered before that what had happened to me as a little girl was called sex. I had buried it all so deeply inside me for so long hoping it would just go away. I wanted the reality of my life to just go away. I wanted someone else's life, not mine.

I woke in intensive care the next day. I almost died, I was angry I hadn't.

◎ Workout 3

Reality overload

I have spent many years in denial. It was an important phase of my life – it kept me alive. It was an effective coping mechanism when I had no other.

◎ ◎ ◎ ◎ ◎

Coping with reality takes emotional skill and support. I am a work in progress, on my reality trainer wheels. I will remember to be patient and kind to myself as I commence to build my emotional fitness.

◎ ◎ ◎ ◎ ◎

Too much reality can be like too much sunlight for someone who has spent years in a darkened room. They need time to slowly adjust. They will lose their ability to see and become temporarily blinded by the light if it is suddenly forced upon them.

◎ ◎ ◎ ◎ ◎

A key to healing and moving out of denial or fantasy into reality is to go at my own pace. I am not a bad person because of my denial; I have been wounded and I am now choosing to heal.

◎ ◎ ◎ ◎ ◎

I will let others know if they are going too fast for me. It is my responsibility to honour myself if I begin to feel overwhelmed. People who attempt to force me to go at their pace and shame me if I am unable to may not understand that I am in healing. I will not assume that others will slow down for me. I must ask them to do so and explain what is comfortable to share with them.

◎ ◎ ◎ ◎ ◎

> **I can avoid reality overload today with phrases such as:**
> *I am new at this … I don't want to rush things … Please just give me some time … Could you slow down, you are going too fast for me … I need some time out … I will have to get back to you.*

Now go to the back of the book, and photocopy and fill in the 'Personal Progress' page.

4. Receiving respect

Receiving feels wrong and uncomfortable, like disinfectant
on a wound.

Cynthia Morton

I had mastered unplugging my heart since the incident with Harry, and promiscuity became a way of life. I was now about eighteen and had decided that I was good for only one thing with men so I might as well get used to it.

I attracted emotional sharks. I knew how to handle abuse and with the right amount of alcohol I didn't feel a thing.

'Can I take you out then? Will you come?' he yelled because the night-club music was so loud.

'Yeah, sure, why not … here's my address', I said, writing my name and address on the back of a soggy beer coaster.

I had my eye on someone else. I knew this guy would never show so I handed him the coaster and made my way through the smoky crowded room.

A week passed. It was 7 p.m. and there was a knock at the door. I was going out, still unsure as to where, but it was Friday night. I never spent Friday nights at home.

It was probably the next-door neighbour wanting my mother for something. I was annoyed at the inconvenience. Mum was not home and I was not feeling very sociable. I opened the door with a pretend smile.

'Sorry if I'm a little early, I can wait in the car if you're not ready yet', he said nervously.

I was stunned. It was the guy from last week who I gave my address to on the soggy coaster. He had mentioned something about a restaurant and 7 p.m. next Friday but I had just nodded not really believing a word he said. What was he so nervous about? I was confused. He was not my type – a bit shy – actually he was definitely not my type when I noticed he was wearing a tie.

'Ah, yeah, just give me a sec', I said as I left him standing at the door while I grabbed my shoes. I had nothing else to do tonight, and I could give him the slip later after he had paid for me to get into the nightclub and bought me a few drinks.

We pulled up outside a little restaurant. 'This is the place I was telling you about', he said proudly. 'The food is really good.'

We were actually going out for dinner. I was pleasantly surprised. I had never been on a date before; this must be a real date, I thought to myself.

As we were seated at our table I began to feel uncomfortable – the rose on the table, the little candle gently burning, the waiter pulling out the chair for me. I felt awkward; I was being treated like a lady.

He wanted to chat and make eye contact while we spoke. I was used to dimly lit, smoky nightclubs where no conversation was possible or necessary, and eye contact was kept to a minimum. I kept looking up at the ceiling and all around the room. My cleavage was up around my throat. Why wasn't he looking at that, I wondered. I drank the champagne as quickly as I could, waiting for my 'beer goggle' vision. I could look anyone in the eye with a certain amount of alcohol in my system. My focus would be poor but it would seem like I was looking at them, even though it was an amphibian-like glazed stare.

The main course had just been cleared away. He had ordered a second bottle of champagne for me. He had not yet finished his first glass, I was on my fifth.

'Are you going to have a dessert? This is my treat tonight, I would really like it if you would let me pay', he said in such a gentlemanly way.

I was immediately suspicious. As far as I knew all men were sharks. They did not give unless they got.

'Hmm, I bet he wants a quickie on the way home', I thought to myself.

'Yeah sure, let's have a look, what have they got', I slurred, picking up the menu and scanning it for the most expensive dessert.

We ordered dessert and then he drove me home. He did not stop or ask to go parking on the way. When we pulled up outside my home he did not pause but got out of the car straightaway and came around to open my door. He walked me up the driveway, gently helping me as I stumbled in my high heels. We were standing at the front door when he asked me if he could kiss me goodnight.

'Are you gay?' I thought to myself, but said nothing. I smiled at him in a state of confusion as he softly kissed me on the cheek.

'I had a really great night tonight, Cindy, can I give you a call?' he asked as he walked towards the driveway.

I nodded, very confused at being driven home by 11 p.m. on a Friday night.

The next morning as I walked towards my pale blue VW beetle to drive to work I noticed a long-stemmed red rose under my windscreen wiper.

'This guy's a stalker', I thought to myself. I was very uncomfortable. I felt physically sick and afraid. I did not know how to have a relationship with my own heart let alone anyone else's, especially a male's.

He was a dolphin male who had treated me respectfully, like a lady. I had to think of him as a desperate loser. How could he want me? I had no self-respect and therefore could not receive it from anyone else. It would have been like trying to feed a newborn baby a steak dinner. It would be impossible – a child has no teeth to chew the meat. I had no teeth of self-respect. I was in dire need of the protein but unable to process it.

He called, and it terrified me. I never saw him again.

◎ Workout 4

Receiving respect

I sometimes get angry when people are being nice to me because it can be so uncomfortable. It feels like they are cleaning my fear-based wounds with love, and it stings. But it is good for me, so today I will try not to wince and pull away.

Other times I get suspicious because they are being respectful. I wonder what they want from me. I will remember today that there are sharks and dolphins on the planet. Some people give to get and others give because they sincerely enjoy it. I am not obliged to another just because they treat me respectfully.

I know I enjoy giving to people I care about and respect. I am grateful to the people in my life whom I respect. They are role models and show me how to live life with meaning and integrity. I like to watch them. Sometimes it's quite difficult for me to tell them how I feel about them. When they look at me, warmly smile and say thank you, I feel good, as if I have given them a small gift. If they dismiss my words, I feel misunderstood or as if they are not accepting my gift. If others show me signs of respect today I will say thank you, appreciating that it may be a confronting task for them to speak about how they feel.

A balanced life is about giving and receiving. It is selfish to deprive others of the opportunity to give to me. Receiving homework is difficult; I will not hide from it today.

I will remember that I deserve to be treated with respect and dignity today.

◎ ◎ ◎ ◎ ◎

Possible responses when others are treating me with respect today:
Thank you … I appreciate you telling me that … It's great to feel useful, thank you … It's my pleasure.

5. Running away from self

The real act of discovery is not in finding new lands, but in seeing with new eyes.

Marcel Proust

The man sending me bottles of French champagne was smiling at me. He was in his late forties and quite unattractive but he was a distraction. I was nineteen years old and addicted to distractions now. I was on the run – from myself.

It was 1981 and the nightclub scene in Sydney was pumping. I had sold my car in Brisbane two days before to a guy at my local garage and used the money to fly away.

I had been in a kind of relationship with an Australian Wallaby rugby player over the past few months. We did not speak much, but had a lot of sex after his football games; it was the closest thing to a relationship I had experienced to date. But he had just dumped me – on a football tour to New Zealand he had found someone else. So I decided I needed to run, to get away. Brisbane was too small; Sydney sounded like the place to be.

I was in the Sydney Hilton nightclub with a girl I had only just met. We were on the prowl. I was out to find a man to use, to hurt. I wanted to win for once; I wanted to have the power. The older guy sending us the champagne had earned my attention.

The delicious bubbles of champagne were like intimate friends to me. They helped me escape from myself. New town, new life, new me, I had decided.

He had also sent over some strawberries. I placed one between my lips and bit down hard on it holding eye contact with him. His friend was a famous racing car driver. I had seen him on television. They both headed towards our booth and asked if they could join us. We smiled our consent.

'I fly back to London in a few days. Have you ever been there?' He sounded like Prince Charles. His name was Roger.

'No, I haven't but would love to go, trouble is I don't know anyone over there', I answered, knowing this man was an international traveller who wasn't short of a buck.

'Well, maybe we could help each other out', he teased as he placed his soft, pale hand on my thigh.

I wanted to find out what he was willing to deal for a night of sex with me. I found him extremely unattractive and had never had sex with any male prior to this night who I did not consider a 'trophy'. Trophy men needed to be physically attractive first and foremost. But after listening to this man speak about his work I knew that the assets he had were not physical but material and in this case I was willing to make an exception.

Roger was the managing director of a famous French fashion house. He was based in Mayfair, London, and travelled the world. He was in Australia seeing a famous Sydney socialite who stocked his label in her exclusive boutiques as well as other Australian buyers. Sleeping with this man would, I knew, be intolerable sober – I found him quite revolting. So I made him an offer with the help of my friend who was a businesswoman. While we were in the ladies toilet she suggested that if I were to sleep with him he was to give me a return ticket to London and put it in writing, and she would witness it.

I did not care if he said no and frankly was surprised when he agreed to it. We got some Hilton letterhead from reception and he wrote that he would agree to buy me a return ticket and signed his name, and then so did I and my friend. He then offered me work in the London office as a secretary once he found out that I could do shorthand and typing. I agreed. I did not have the necessary paperwork to do this so he also agreed to fly me to the Australian Embassy in Canberra the next day with a letter from his company requesting my services in London immediately. The deal was made and in writing. I then needed more champagne to get as drunk as I could. A part of me had crossed a border within myself that I had never crossed before. I deliberately shut my heart off. I had learnt how to do it to protect myself as a little girl with Dad and the man next door and it had subconsciously happened with Harry, but I had never deliberately done it before. It was like flicking a switch and the lights around my heart and soul went out.

Unfortunately I still recall flashes of that revolting night. He was a short, narrow-shouldered, white-skinned Englishman. He had no muscle in his behind, and a muscular bottom was always a prerequisite for the men I chose. His hair was very fair and his eyelashes were almost white. The skin around his eyes seemed pink, like a pig's, and his touch was like that of a dead fish. His body smell was stale and as I type these words I feel like dry retching.

But I did the deed and flew to Canberra the next day. I felt empowered by the secret I held over him and finally felt that sex was something that I could use to get what I wanted rather than have it taken from me. Now that I knew how to turn my heart off I felt as though I had been given the keys to a fast car – I could go where I wanted and get what I wanted, and it felt safer than caring. But I felt unclean and dirtier inside than I ever had before. Sexual encounters prior to Roger had involved at least some hope, honesty or true desire and even though they had all ended in disappointment because I chose only sharks I never felt as dirty inside as I did that day.

On the trip to London I read Erica Jong's book, *Fear of Flying*. I had no idea who she was and little of what the book was about and I remember struggling with my dyslexia while trying to read it. But what I understood, I loved.

When I arrived at Heathrow airport in London one of Roger's impeccably dressed, well-spoken staff greeted me. She was petite, elegant and polite. Next to her I felt like a hippopotamus. My hair was bleached blonde and a mess from sleeping on the flight. My clothes looked cheap and nasty compared with her well-fitted, crisp, no-nonsense suit. I was wearing a baby-pink angora jumper that was two sizes too small. My double D cup breasts were squashed and misshapen underneath the jumper. My white, Gold Coast-style surfie skirt looked like a crushed pillowcase and I felt extremely awkward to be me. My voice had become very raspy from the long flight, so talking was difficult, and frankly I did not have much to say for myself. I felt that as soon as she looked at me she knew what I had done to get this flight. Her name was Anna and she was a clean, proper woman, I was a dirty, inappropriate one.

I had run all the way from Australia to London. Trouble was, I had taken something with me that I was so desperate to escape from – me.

◎ Workout 5

Running away from self

I now understand that trying to escape or run away from myself does not work, for wherever I go I take me with me.

◎ ◎ ◎ ◎ ◎

Drugs, alcohol, food, sex, exercise, work, spending and co-dependent relationships don't work either. They just put my pain on pause and create more problems. I know that the older I get the harder it becomes to avoid my issues. I will need to keep increasing my external distractions to distract myself from my internal pain.

◎ ◎ ◎ ◎ ◎

Tolerating how I feel, being still and not running from myself is my emotional homework for today. Happy feelings can be just as challenging as difficult feelings, and sometimes they are harder.

◎ ◎ ◎ ◎ ◎

Sometimes running away from love and success is just as much an issue as avoiding pain. I will be aware of this and make sure I do not hide from love and success today – I am worthy. I am aware that in the past I have sabotaged good things, or taken them away from myself, as a form of control. This seems to be easier to deal with than having someone else take away love or success. If I feel the urge to wreck something healthy that I am building for myself, I will ask for help or time out today and allow the feeling to pass through me.

◎ ◎ ◎ ◎ ◎

Pain is a part of life. The saying that 'pain is inevitable but suffering is optional' will help me today. Suffering is about the judgement I put around my pain. I will remember that if pain surfaces for me today I am not being punished – and that in every crisis there is a gift. It has been said before that 'pain is the gift that nobody wants'. I will remember that with every painful experience I have had in life there have been gifts and things to learn about myself.

◎ ◎ ◎ ◎ ◎

Actions I can take to avoid running away from myself today:

Ask for help ... Write about it ... Cry about it ... Let someone who cares about me hold me ... Take time out for myself.

6. Smother mothers

I treated my children like projects, efficiently managing and orchestrating their lives, often at the expense of their feelings.

Ellen Sue Stern

I met Joe shortly after I had returned from London. Australia seemed so good once I was on the other side of the globe. As soon as I arrived at Heathrow I wanted to return home; it was too cold for me. I spent a few lost weeks hitchhiking through Europe in an alcoholic blackout, found my way to Frankfurt airport, returned to Sydney and then hitchhiked back to Brisbane.

Roger was a memory I was desperate to erase and so I immersed myself back into Australian nightlife looking for that perfect man to take me away and save me – from myself.

Joe was it. A tall, blonde, sun-drenched Australian male – and a clever one at that. Private schoolboy who was university educated. He had a gentle nature and loved drugs as I loved alcohol. We were a perfect match.

We lived together for a few years and then eventually married in 1986. It was my twenty-third year of life, he was twenty-five. He had inherited the family home, which enabled us to start a family straightaway. I was pregnant with our first child within three months.

Our first son, Sam, was born early in 1987 and Mitchell late in 1988. I had managed to stop drinking during both pregnancies, and stayed sober during their early childhood, but became drunk on motherhood.

The boys were the most divine beings I had ever encountered.

I was like a mother tiger around them. I smothered them with my fear of something happening to them. They did not learn to ride bikes until quite late in life because I was too scared to have them ride too far away from me. Neither of them played team sports partially because Joe and I were both so hung over every weekend that we knew it was a commitment neither of us could keep – it would have hindered our partying. But it was also because I was afraid of something happening to them.

I was the sort of mother who did not know how to pull back and leave them be to find the dignity and wisdom we do when we make our own mistakes. When a problem presented itself in their lives I thought it was my job to remove the problem for them. I saw it as a huge boulder being placed in the pathway of their lives and would hire a huge crane to come and remove the hurdle they had to face instead of allowing them the opportunity to learn how to climb over it for themselves. I would then hire a landscaper to come and fill in the hole and plant flowers for them. They did not get the chance to tend to their lives' own paths.

When they needed validation or love, I would overcompensate and drown them. Instead of sprinkling water on them to nourish them, as you do with little flower seedlings, I would pour a whole bucket on them and leave them spluttering for air, uprooting them. I was out of balance totally and doing more damage than good.

Once the children were both at school I realised I did not have a life. I had been using food as a drug and was uncomfortably overweight. When Mitchell started school I began crash dieting and lost over 20 kilograms. I started using diet pills again, laxatives, and drugs with my husband, took up cigarette smoking and re-established myself as a Barbie.

It was not until I had left Joe and was in early recovery in 1996 that I really began to understand how I had disempowered the boys with my fear.

Because of my fear of violence I had forbidden them to hit each other and shamed them if they ever did. I had always told them to use their words, not their fists. But I now understand that there are times in a male's life when you do have to assert yourself and set boundaries, and sometimes that involves being physical. Young boys are like lion cubs; they need to use their bodies and wrestle to find their strength.

It was early in 1996 when Sam asked me to really listen to him. 'Mum, I think there is something wrong. When I am playing rugby and someone unjustly biffs me, my instinct is to protect myself and hit them back, but I can't. I get really upset about it. I've got to be able to protect myself sometimes, Mum', he said, almost pleading with me not to judge him and make him a bad person, as I so often did with anyone who got into a punch-up.

One afternoon we were driving home from school, both boys in the back of the car, when I passed two high school boys having a fight. I stopped the car, got out and stood between them to break up the fight. Both of the boys slunk down in their seats so they could not be seen. I had embarrassed them immensely and the two boys fighting told me in no uncertain terms to back off as it had nothing to do with me.

I got some expert advice on how to help Sam and we eventually got a punching bag and tied it up underneath our house. Many an afternoon I would stand in the kitchen peeling potatoes while the whole house seemed to shake around me. Sam now had a way to let out years of pent-up natural testosterone that I had forbidden him to release.

Mitchell had difficulty with sport. Because no-one had ever encouraged him to use his body as a young boy, during his teenage years he found he had no ball or running skills whatsoever. I began to really see how I had deprived him of learning about himself. Falling over and skinning our knees to gain confidence in how to use our bodies is so essential in the formative years, and both my boys missed out on this. In rowing Mitchell has now found a sport that he enjoys but it took a great deal of courage for him to even try out because of his lack of confidence and my contagious fear that something terrible could happen to him.

It was also around this time that I stopped controlling and dictating what I wanted them to wear. It was so hard the very first time I did it. I remember it as if it were yesterday. We were in a discount clothing store. I was still on a pension and money was tight. I was looking at some things for myself and the boys were bored. I noticed a rack that had men's Hawaiian shirts for $10. I told them that they could each pick out one for themselves while I finished my shopping.

'I love this one, Mum', Mitchell said, holding a bold blue floral print shirt up to his chest.

'I like it too, Mitch. Good choice! Sam, have you found one?'

'Yep, this is way cool, I want this one', Sam said, smiling and holding up a shirt that looked like a car accident had happened on it. It was red, with some yellow, and frankly I thought it was hideous.

'You're not wearing that, Sam, it's revolting. Find something else, there are heaps of nice ones to choose from', I demanded in my authoritarian tone without even thinking.

'Well, Mum, don't say I can choose one, when I can't. You want me to choose what you like, you don't care about what I like', he said, annoyed that I had been so condescending and not considered his feelings at all.

I stood there as the shop assistant smiled in anticipation of an argument. I ignored her. I really heard him for the first time. Until then, what they wore was about my ego and what others thought about how my children looked. It was killing his individuality – he felt oppressed because he was.

I was looking at a budding young man not a boy any more. I hated men who were still controlled by their mothers, and I was creating that type of male in my own son by my controlling ego and insecurity.

'Mum, I think it's cool too. It would look good on Sam', Mitch gently defended his brother.

Mitchell had always been a bit of a fashion guru, and he did have a developed eye for style and colour. Sam had a different approach to clothes, a nonchalant, whatever he felt like sort of style.

'I'm sorry, Sam; I did go back on my word. If you like it, sweetheart, we'll get it. You will have to be patient with me, I am still getting used to the fact that you are both young men now, not little boys', I said apologetically.

Sam seemed to straighten his body, pleased that he had spoken up for himself and had his needs met.

'Cool, thanks Mum', he said as he placed the loud shirt on the counter.

'Well done', the shop assistant quietly whispered to me. 'I have a young son and I really learnt from how you handled that', she said sincerely.

'Can I wear it now?' Sam asked as he headed towards the change room.

He wore that shirt nonstop all summer. He loved it, and so did I for what it showed me about myself.

 Workout 6

Smother mothers

I will have compassion for myself or my mother if at times smother mothering has been a part of my life.

People sometimes use relationships as a type of drug to help fill an emotional void inside them. Mothers smother because they do not have a secure sense of self. They get their self-esteem from being a mother. This is hazardous for everyone's emotional health.

When a mother attaches her self-worth to her child, her child ceases to be an individual and instead becomes a resource for validation of her existence. Her ability to consider her child's feelings above her own is impaired.

Smother mothers are a type of workaholic. They become obsessive with their work, which is parenting, and lose balance in other relationships.

If I become controlling or obsessive with my children it is an indicator that I am out of balance. It is healthy for my children to disagree and have different tastes and opinions from me. I did from my mother. One of us does not have to be wrong. It is a healthy sign if my child feels safe enough to speak up for themselves when their opinions or tastes don't match mine.

I can best help my mother with smother love by not enabling her to control me. If I feel powerless to disagree with my mother I may need some professional help.

Smother mother recovery reminders:

I can disagree with my mother respectfully today ... It is a sign of my children's emotional health if they can assert their differing opinions and tastes with me without fear ... It is not my job to become emotionally responsible for my mother's insecurities.

7. Following intuition

Intuition is a spiritual faculty and does not explain, but simply points the way.

Florence Scovel Shinn

It was a hot summer day late in 1990. I was driving my husband's ute over the Indooroopilly Bridge in Brisbane. I was having trouble finding a radio station that played music I wanted to listen to. Joe and I had such different taste in music.

'MMMFM your kind of music.' Ah, I had found my station finally.

I was looking forward to picking up some big floor cushions I was having made in pale blue gingham for Mitchell's room. I was on my own. It was a Saturday morning and Joe had been working in the garden with the boys who were covered in mud and having a delightful time with him, so I left them to enjoy the time together and jumped at the chance of some time for myself.

The house where I was going was not far away. The radio crackled as the announcer said, *'Earthwatch and the Smithsonian Institute are running a competition. Write in and tell us what you think about the green movement and how you can help the planet. We want to hear from you, and the prize is a trip for two to the Amazon jungle in Peru, trekking with scientists from the Smithsonian on their expedition …'*

My heart pumped. I could see Joe standing next to a huge tree that disappeared into the canopy. He had a khaki shirt on, and I was taking his photo. I saw it as clear as day. I knew we would be going. The adrenalin pumping through my being was overwhelming. I rushed to pick up the cushions and sped home. I had to write. We were going to the Amazon: I knew it so deeply within myself that it frightened me and I felt like I needed to cry.

'That was quick', Joe said with surprise as I unloaded the cushions from the car. 'I thought you'd be another few hours. The boys are fine – you didn't have to hurry back', he assured me.

I could not speak. I smiled and raced up the driveway. I grabbed a foolscap notepad and a pen and sat out on the deck. My hand was in a frenzy, writing. I had to tell them about Mother Nature, my parent, and how I believed in colour and our energy centres. I had attended a course on crystal healing not long before and had learnt a great deal about colour and the human chakras. While some of it was a little complex for me, the basics made sense. Green is the colour of the heart chakra, and pink is a secondary colour. I knew that the Amazon jungle from the air is the shape of a heart.

It was as plain as day to me that humans were attacking their own hearts – myself included – and that Mother Nature's heart, which was represented by the green Amazon, was also being attacked, almost as though the earth was physically manifesting what humans were doing to themselves.

I was sober at this point in my life and had been writing a book. My working title was 'Emotional Fitness' and I explained that I needed to visit Mother Nature's heart in the Amazon, that she was calling me.

'What are you doing? Who are you writing to?' Joe asked as he placed a cup of tea and a packet of biscuits on the table.

'I'm going to the Amazon. Do you want to come? Do you want me to write that you will be coming with me?' I quickly questioned as I looked up from the notepad, pen poised, waiting for a response.

'What? What are you talking about? Do you even know where the Amazon is?' Joe responded, humouring my conviction. He knew I had no geographical knowledge, that my educational level was poor, and he was right. I had no idea where the Amazon was. It didn't matter – I was going.

'Do you want to come or not?' I was insulted.

He smiled and with a playful attitude replied, 'Yeah, sure, why not? I'll come along, but don't get your hopes up – thousands of people will enter a competition like that.'

Two weeks later our telephone rang while we were playing Scrabble on a Sunday evening. I answered, and when a voice told me that I had won and been chosen out of thousands of entrants to go to the Amazon on this trek I cried. I wanted to say that I knew I was going because I had seen myself there in a vision but I did not think anyone would believe me. I even doubted my own knowing for it seemed too uncanny. How could I have known?

So a month or so later we were off. Joe had never left Australia before this trip so I was very pleased to be able to do this trip with him. We had to leave our boys behind, which was my only concern as during our time away Mitchell would turn two. I was very sad about missing that, but knew I had to go.

On arriving in South America and meeting the scientists I immediately felt inadequate. Joe had a science degree and spoke freely with them. I discovered Jungle Juice, which the natives made. It was an alcoholic drink, clear like vodka but smelling like methylated spirits. It helped me be with Joe. He was straight for the first time ever in our marriage. Taking drugs over the Colombian border was not an option. We did not get along when he was straight, so Jungle Juice saved the day.

We were out on a morning walk in the depths of the Amazon when it hit me. I stood still and looked at the beauty and nature around me, the wonder – it was almost as if I could hear Mother Nature's heart beating. I looked further down the path and saw Joe standing in front of a huge tree that was so tall it disappeared into the canopy.

'Take my photo – it will be a good shot. Look at the size of the trunk of this tree, it must be hundreds of years old', Joe said in sheer amazement. As I looked through the camera lens at Joe in his khaki shirt I was reminded of the vision I had while driving his ute a few months before. The path was exactly the same as I had seen it. It was as though something was telling me I was right, that I could trust this knowing, this intuition, and it did not matter if it made sense to anyone else or not. It was my gift for me to listen to and it would guide me if I did to wondrous places such as this.

On Mitchell's second birthday I fretted like a mother dog for her pups. My body, my breasts, my womb and my heart ached for my child. I spent the day in a foetal ball on the balsa wood makeshift floor amongst the thick undergrowth. We were six hours up the Amazon River from a town called Iquitos.

The day after Mitchell's birthday I felt drained emotionally. I had cried so much that I had no energy left. I was numb and just wanted to go home. My eyes were like swollen red tomatoes, my eyelids so puffy they almost hurt. So I did what I always do when I need to help myself – I wrote.

I sat alone on the thatch-roofed timber boat as we quietly coasted up the Amazon to a new exploration site. My pad was on my lap and I was writing to myself, words that I cannot even recall today, but they were consoling words of silent poetry to the sadness in me to soothe my heart. The others were all clustered up the other end of the boat listening to the scientist explain yet another fascinating fact about this sacred place we were in. It was then that I instinctively looked up from my pad as if someone had nudged my shoulder. I looked over the side of the boat into the almost black deep water of the Amazon. I experienced one of the most beautiful things I have ever seen during my time on this earth. Even today as I type these words doubt lurks within me that it is even true, for it was so glorious.

A face appeared out of the water and looked straight at me. It was the head of a pink dolphin. I had never seen anything so beautiful other than my newborn children in all my life. Its snout looked as though it had been spray painted with a silvery pink glitter spray, something you would see in a Walt Disney children's movie. It silently looked at me for only a short time and then turned its head slightly as if it were looking at the others further up the boat. I have since learnt that pink dolphins are only found in the Amazon and have vertebrae in their neck or head that helps them turn it. It seemed to look back at me and then it slid back into the still water and disappeared. I was in shock. I was rendered mute. As soon as it left I doubted I had even seen it. I looked up at the others to see if they had seen it, that perhaps there was a pod swimming around the boat, but no-one said anything at all. They were listening to the scientist explain something about plant life.

I wondered if it was real – it was so precious. And why only me, why did no-one else see it?

I said nothing to anyone for years about what I saw. It was only when I became clean and sober that I spoke about it for the first time. I had made friends with a beautiful spiritual Aboriginal man who was also in recovery. His eyes were chocolate and deep, connected to his ancient spirit. I knew he would be safe to tell. As I spoke about this unbelievable dolphin, I cried, and got a tight lump in my throat. I had to swallow hard to say the words; it was difficult to acknowledge that something so exceptionally beautiful had happened to me.

He sat quietly and listened to me and then gently smiled. He understood intuition intimately. He held my hands and looked deep into my eyes. The depth of his gaze was overwhelming. We said nothing to each other, but just sat in the grace of silence.

Following my intuition had led me to a pink dolphin on the other side of the world – it was like living a miracle.

◎ Workout 7
Following intuition

I will be more aware of my intuition today – when my senses tell me whether something is healthy or unhealthy for me. It is sometimes called a 'gut feeling'.

◎ ◎ ◎ ◎ ◎

I can think of my intuitive nature as a set of traffic lights Mother Nature installs in every human being at birth. Red for stop, yellow for caution and green for go. I just need to pay attention to each colour and follow its cue.

◎ ◎ ◎ ◎ ◎

I will remember that excessive use of mind-altering substances will impair my capacity to read the colours, rendering me colour-blind to my own intuition. I will still get a strong feeling but I will be unable to make a move in the healthiest direction as the colour will be indiscernible.

◎ ◎ ◎ ◎ ◎

Following my intuition can seem daunting at times, as it often defies logic. It's really about following my truth and listening to myself to see what feels right for me. I will take time to pause and ask myself if I want to take or not take a certain action today. If I am unsure that it is my yellow light giving me the

caution signal, I may need more time or information before I
can make my choice.

I will not give my power away today and ask others to decide
what is healthiest for me. My choices are my responsibility. As
I cannot know on every level what is right for someone else,
nor can they know that for me.

Intuition reminders for today:
*I can say that I need time to consider a request before
answering … Drugs and alcohol render me colour-blind to my
intuition – I will not make any important decisions if I have
either of these in my system … It is safe to believe in myself.*

8. An emotional Bandaid called denial

Problems are messages.

Shakti Gawain

We returned from the Amazon and life continued as if we had never been away. I began drinking again and Joe resumed his drug habit.

I had written a great deal during my abstinent years of pregnancy and breastfeeding. My manuscript, 'Emotional Fitness', was lengthy. It was autobiographical.

I had written in great detail about colour and the chakras and about motherhood. It was not a lie, nor the truth, but denial. I only wrote about the good bits in my life and when writing about other key people in my life I made them into perfect gods. Faultless!

That was how I lived my life. Our whole life functioned in a state of denial. Not just Joe and I, but our friends and family – we were all great pretenders.

Our friends, Meg and Peter, were a perfect example. Peter was consistently unfaithful to Meg. He travelled internationally with his work and spoke about the topless bars he visited on his travels. Meg would just glaze over and pour herself another gin and tonic. One evening at our place we had several couples over for dinner. It was in the early hours of the morning when I caught Peter kissing Emma, a single friend of mine, outside our toilet. He had his hand on her breast and was in a lustful frenzy. Peter knew I saw him, but continued nonetheless.

Later, Peter and Emma were dirty dancing and I remember marvelling at Meg's capacity to pretend that it just wasn't happening.

'What happens on his trips stays outside the door of this house', she would say defensively if ever I asked her about his playboy lifestyle.

She too was dangerously flirting with her music teacher and the man next door. But to the outside world Meg and Peter had the perfect marriage. European cars, expensive holidays and the best of everything that money could buy.

Joe and I were also living a lie. We were so violent with each other behind closed doors, but we never spoke about our problems on the days following our terrible fights. If either of us was bruised we did not discuss it, we just forgot about it and pretended that it had never happened. I made sure I always sat on his lap and flirted with him in public to keep up appearances. I had learnt that from my mother. Never speak about it, make up lies if there were bruises and keep the family secrets at all costs. Trouble is when you pretend for long enough you can even convince yourself that it's not happening.

I regularly went nightclubbing without Joe – looking for someone better. I would take off my wedding ring and hunt for that perfect man that was going to fix my life. I chose to believe I was so unhappy because Joe wasn't making me happy. It was his fault.

My manuscript was rejected by many publishing houses. No wonder – it had no substance. It was all pretence. It was not until I had my first session with my shrink, Mal, during recovery, years later, that I noticed I had started that manuscript in my late teens. It was as though nothing had happened before that time. I had totally denied my childhood. My life started after my teenage suicide attempt. And even then it included nothing dysfunctional.

Denial is something you don't know you are in. It is very difficult to identify in yourself.

'I deny I have any denial' was a statement I would utter during my using years. I did not know I was an alcoholic and a drug addict. I did not comprehend that I was a survivor of childhood abuse or that I lived with domestic violence. I would not acknowledge that my mother had a serious drinking problem and that all of my relationships while using were based on conforming. I was extremely narrow-minded and afraid, but liked to think of myself as worldly and fearless.

Denial was how I coped with problems. It was like putting heavy plaster around a wound year after year – when the wound seeped, more plaster was applied. The thicker the plaster of denial, the less emotional mobility I had, but at least I was protected from my pain.

I did not understand then that pain is the root of self-knowledge.

◎ Workout 8

An emotional Bandaid called denial

Most people live in denial to some degree. It seems as though it is human nature to deny the greatness that lies within us all.

◎ ◎ ◎ ◎ ◎

To deny my talent, intellect, sexuality, hunger, body shape, pain, insecurities, desires or sadness is to deny my truth.

◎ ◎ ◎ ◎ ◎

Denial has kept me alive and has been a coping mechanism until this phase in my life. It is like a Bandaid that protects a wound. It eventually needs to come off so that the wound can heal. I hurt myself if I keep placing Bandaids over old Bandaids. This compounds my problems and infects them, making them worse than they were in the beginning.

◎ ◎ ◎ ◎ ◎

I used to believe that if I denied my pain that would make it go away. I now understand that I just put it on pause for a later date. It is easier to keep up with my pain than to have to catch up with more than one issue at a later date. Today I choose to deal with any pain as it arises.

◎ ◎ ◎ ◎ ◎

I will remember not to be self-righteous if I see others in denial as I was once. I was helped the most by kindness and compassion, not by shame and harsh judgement.

◎ ◎ ◎ ◎ ◎

Denial awareness for today:
I will be patient with myself today ... I will give time, time ... I am only as sick as the secrets I keep ... I am unafraid of my truth ... Pain is a part of life; it is my denial that makes me suffer unnecessarily.

9. Emotionally medicating

Pain is inevitable, suffering is optional.

Kathleen Casey Theisen

It was June 1995. Our marriage was in tatters. Joe and I were fighting constantly, drinking and using more drugs than we had in over a decade together.

'A boob job is a great idea. It will give you a lift. Why not – you deserve it,' Mum said with enthusiasm.

I hated having sex with Joe. I felt sure it must be because my breasts were not as firm as they used to be. After breastfeeding two boys and years of yo-yo dieting my breasts were sagging and tired. I wore padding in every bra to try and maintain the once full shape of which I was so proud. I was a Miss Wet T-shirt in my heyday – my breasts had given me a great deal of self-worth. I felt sure that new boobs would fix things up.

A week later I was devastated when I found an envelope in the mailbox on which a neighbour had written. A letter sent to me from the breast clinic had accidentally been delivered to her. She had opened it without checking the name, and then realised that it was for me and put it in our mailbox. I was devastated. I was sure that the whole neighbourhood would now know that I was going in for day surgery.

The surgery went well and I was home in the afternoon. The pain-killing drugs were amazing, I ate them like lollies. I was told not to drink after taking them, but of course I ignored that and got drunk that evening. I danced and gyrated around the lounge room, euphoric that my new breasts were going to be the medicine to save my marriage and my self-esteem. I was heavily bandaged and wearing a maternity bra, but nonetheless the next morning I was in excruciating pain. Being so drunk and high on pain-killers and other drugs I felt sure I had torn something inside my breasts while dancing the night before.

I lay around for a few days pretending to girlfriends that I was unwell with the flu. The boys were the hardest to control. They were used to hugs and being picked up and I had to protect myself from their rough play.

'They look wonderful, he's done a good job', said Mum with pride in her voice. I changed into every outfit and bikini I could find, giving her a fashion parade of my new body.

Joe loved them. It suited me fine that they were numb for months. I could not feel his touch, and did not want to. I enjoyed sex again only because I loved looking at my new breasts. I felt like a Playboy centrefold.

In early recovery I wrote this poem that describes my quest to become a perfect Barbie during phases like this.

Sickly Pink Barbie World

Champagne, male attention and approval at any cost
Stalk me now before the moment is lost
Tear at my flesh, as the lion devours the deer
Make me feel worthwhile and help me drown out the fear

Hate them, obsess over me, want me instead of your wife
I'm bored with everything; I hate me and my life
Booze, drugs and surgery to make me just right
We pretend when in public, but we go home and fight

Who is that in the mirror? She is a stranger to me
Eats everything or nothing, to be normal is her plea
Fake tan, fake breasts, fingernails and hair
Yes that's me ... help ... I am numb as I stare

Cigarettes and joints, more chocolate, now a pill
Fix the lipstick, pretend I am happy, my heart wants to kill
The merry-go-round speeds up, how do I get off this ride?
Oh yes, my silent friend is always there
Good old suicide ...

As the months passed, the novelty of my new breasts wore off. I was desperately unhappy; the deep black hole inside myself kept haunting me. I wanted to die, to escape my life. Alcohol was not lifting me like it used to and drugs were only temporary relief.

I organised a big lunch for all my girlfriends. We were all bored with life, and a lunch offered some relief from our pretentious lives. What would we wear, what would we pretend to eat, who could we flirt with, where would we want to be seen?

I wore a red designer dress. It had a fitted waist and showed off my new breasts brilliantly. I took some speed before I went to lunch and drank and smoked the day away, vomiting up my lunch to maintain my flat stomach.

Most of the other girls had gone home. It was 7 p.m. in the evening and I had phoned Joe with some lie telling him I couldn't get away. I made friends with the sister of a woman I did not like or know very well. She was drunk like me. Her name was Susie. We were both slurring our words but complimenting each other on how sober and divine we looked. The bar staff were rolling their eyes with boredom at our pathetic lustful advances.

'I've just started dating this guy and I'm supposed to meet him after this function. I'll call and see what time he will be ready before we order another round of drinks', Susie said as she held her mobile phone to her ear.

'I'm with a friend, can she come too?' Susie asked the guy on the other end of the phone raising her eyebrows at me with excitement.

'Okay, hang on, I'll just get a pen. Got a pen?' she asked the barman.

Shortly after, we were in a cab and on our way to meet her new guy at an address written on a drink coaster. I think she was grateful for my back-up as she didn't know him very well. She explained that he was actually at his boss's house, but the function had turned into a party now and we were welcome.

His boss was obviously a wealthy man. Electronic steel gates opened for us after Susie spoke into the intercom. We opted to walk down the long driveway that was lined each side with a huge row of palms. The house was a mansion.

'I'm busting to pee, got to do a wee, Susie', I said as I pulled my beautiful red dress up around my waist. I squatted next to one of the palm trees and urinated all over my shoes.

Susie started to laugh, and so did I. I gave myself a bit of a jiggle and pulled up my stockings. We staggered arm-in-arm down the long driveway.

We were yelling and cat-calling as we entered the foyer of the mansion. A butler escorted us to a luxurious entertainment area. The man who owned the house was a man I used to flirt with on a regular basis.

'Robbie, how are you, gorgeous, what are you doing here?' I yelled at him across the room. A woman pulled at his elbow; it was his wife. It was their house, and his mother's wake – they had buried her earlier that day. I don't remember much else except two young guys coming up to me, one grabbing each arm and escorting me to the front door. I passed a television camera that monitored that long driveway; they had all seen me take a pee prior to entering.

'What are you doing, I was invited here, let go of me', I yelled indignantly. 'I am a married woman, don't push me', I threatened.

'You need to leave now, you are not wanted here, and Rob has asked us to get rid of you', one of the guys said firmly, enjoying the power he had been given to humiliate me further.

I became aggressive and threw my champagne glass onto the paved driveway. There were many people standing watching. They had called a cab and pushed me into it, throwing my shoes that I had lost in the scuffle in after me. One of the guys gave the driver $20 and said, 'Just get her out of here; take her home – wherever that is'.

I came to the next morning remembering fragments of the previous night's events. I had lost control. Medicating on drugs and alcohol used to solve all my problems, but these days it just created more.

◎ Workout 9

Emotionally medicating

I will be aware of any pain that arises today and deal with it rather than running from it or medicating with some external substance or distraction. Avoiding pain just creates a huge backlog to deal with at a later date. Medicating with any substance only provides temporary relief and often creates more problems.

◎ ◎ ◎ ◎ ◎

If I need help dealing with any painful issues today, I will seek help. I don't have to deal with my pain on my own.

◎ ◎ ◎ ◎ ◎

I will choose the company of others who are like-minded when dealing with my own pain. Support groups or dolphin people are the best company for me when I am in pain.

◎ ◎ ◎ ◎ ◎

Substances such as drugs, alcohol, binge eating and/or starving, sex addiction or one-night stands, or obsessive cleaning, exercise or work are all areas to be aware of as pain avoiders.

◎ ◎ ◎ ◎ ◎

I will not judge others who choose to medicate but rather show compassion for them, being sure to respect myself and not enable them to abuse or disrespect me because I have chosen a different path. I will not abuse or disrespect them either.

◎ ◎ ◎ ◎ ◎

Alternatives to emotionally medicating today:
Go for a walk … Have a cry … Call your dolphin … Just sit and be still … Write about it … Ask for help.

10. Asking for help – the beginning of the end

I have had enough.

Golda Meir

I was vacuuming the house in my usual routine way when my nicotine cravings became really apparent to me. I could no longer do the whole house without stopping for a cigarette break halfway through. Cigarettes had become one of my lovers. I would sneak away for a rendezvous with them more often than I let on to others. What a relief they offered … I loved them!

My large wine glass winked at me as if to say 'Time for a top up' as I ironed my sheer white top that looked divine over the new French white lacy bra I had just bought. I would wear that tonight at the dinner party we were going to at our neighbour's. Peter was a bosom man; I just loved his hungry eyes on my body. Meg still had no idea that my perfect melon breasts were the result of secret surgery. She loved Joe's attention also, so it was a fair playing field – she had the legs, I had the breasts.

I had fed the boys fish fingers for dinner and had bathed and dressed them in their pyjamas; they were excited and ready to go. We all loved going to Meg's and Peter's house. They had two boys the same age as our sons so everyone had a good time.

I had been drinking since about noon to prepare for the night ahead. It was around 6 p.m. when I escorted my wine glass to the bathroom for my shower. I balanced my precious glass on the shelf above the shower as I undressed so that I could reach it while in the shower. My hand glided across my flat, starving stomach. As I lathered my fake-tanned torso I felt pleased with myself. I reviewed my dietary intake for the day. Only two wafer biscuits, two and a half packets of cigarettes, countless cups of coffee and Diet Coke, half a bottle of tequila with a dash of soda. Well done! My calorie count was deliciously low. I felt empowered by the control I had over my body. My head and heart were chaotic, but my body I controlled. It was my tool, my weapon, a great emotional distraction and I knew how to use it.

I ate enough at dinner to look normal, but discreetly disappeared to the toilet.

'I need a young, young man to drive away those middle-aged blues.' Meg was dancing with herself, eyes closed, and singing at the top of her voice. Her gin and tonics had kicked in.

Joe and Peter were out on the back deck sucking back on a fat joint, discussing the Wallabies' latest win in Rugby Union. The timing was right. I efficiently stuck my finger at that magic spot at the back of my throat and immediately everything I had eaten streamed into the toilet bowl. I did it silently and quickly – a true professional. I checked my lipstick and eyeliner in the mirror – not a smudge. Now for dessert!

Hours had passed and it was around 2 a.m. I had drunk myself sober and the drugs had not given me a high at all – when it happened again. My sewage plug came out and I started to fill up from the inside. The last time this had happened I was sixteen years of age. It was my first suicide attempt. I had overdosed in a toilet block and was so angry when I woke up in intensive care – how I had wanted to die back then. And it was the same now but I was 33. I just wanted to cut myself to let the sewage out. It was flooding my insides. I could taste it in my throat. I so desperately wanted to get out of my own skin.

'Come with me, I need you', I sleazily demanded.

Joe was looking at me through glassy eyes. He smiled and got up from the table and followed me to the bathroom. We did this often – had sex in other people's bathrooms and even in ladies' toilets at weddings. It used to be a thrill and an effective physical distraction from my emotional reality, but for me these days after almost fourteen years together, it no longer gave me the same adrenalin rush. But I needed a physical escape from myself and drugs and alcohol had let me down tonight – again. I made all the appropriate groans and loud noises as Joe went on remote control, to entertain the others still sitting at the table, but felt nothing – I was emotionally dead.

I don't recall what followed; all I know is that I must have passed out some time later. I came to next morning at around 10 a.m. I was naked and had no idea where my clothes were. My body was badly bruised and I didn't know why, and my jaw was really sore – I could hardly move it.

My hair was matted and full of leaves and vomit. I stood up to make my way to the toilet as alcohol-related diarrhoea involuntarily made its way down my inner thigh. I looked at my face in the bathroom mirror and saw this drawn woman with bruised eyes looking back at me – she looked like a raccoon. I knew what that bruising was from – violent, self-induced vomiting. It happened often when I was in blackout. I would make myself vomit so much that I would break all the tiny blood vessels around my eyes.

I cleaned myself up and sat back on the bed. I held onto my knees and started to rock my naked bruised body. I wanted to die. I wanted to go home to that place on the other side of the sky where the sparrows and stars lived.

My dear friend, Mother Nature, was smiling at me through the beautiful tree that stood outside our bedroom window. That tree was a good friend of mine. I spoke to it often. She understood me and watched over me. Her branches were like long limbs that cradled the windows of our bedroom. With those elegant arms, she also held up the boys' tyre swing. She would swing them for hours. I often looked up at her bringing my babies so much joy and silently thanked her. I knew she heard me. She was a white gum tree and to touch her smooth skin with my open palm was a spiritual experience. Her bark was sleek like a white palomino's coat. She was my ally.

I had picked a spot on the South East Freeway near our home that would be perfect to drive my car off into the Brisbane River. I had been thinking about it for weeks. Ending it all; freeing myself from the stench of the sewage of my emotional reality from which I could no longer escape. My buddies, drugs and alcohol, had called it a day. They had given me their best over the decades, but my truth was stronger; it could not be anaesthetised any longer.

But how could I leave this planet and leave my babies here with all those sharks? Who would take care of them? I trusted no-one. I had been entertaining the thought of taking them with me. I understood parents who ended their lives and took their children with them. It seemed responsible to me in my deep state of insanity and desperation. I had envisaged the water level rising up the car windows as the seductive touch of death relieved me of this hell on earth – no-one would get to us in time, it was the perfect plan, we would all be safer off this planet.

The house was silent. Joe had taken the boys to school. I kept seeing their beautiful faces in my mind's eye. Those boys deserved a life. I could not leave them, nor end their lives, but how could I stay? I had no idea how to do life straight.

'I can't do it any more', I sobbed as I confided in my beautiful tree, looking up at her for understanding, 'I don't know how'. I put my head on my knees and the hot tears trickled down my calves. 'Will you help me … please?' I begged my majestic leafy friend.

That conversation between myself and Mother Nature took place on 12 October 1995. I just remember feeling a deep sense of peace and relief that morning after asking her for help. I cried for a long time – then eventually just knew what to do next. I called a help line and found out where to go to get help.

I have not picked up a drink or drug from that day to this.

Thank you, Mother Nature, for hearing my call.

◎ Workout 10

Asking for help – the beginning of the end

If I had been in an almost fatal car accident and broken both legs and arms, I would accept that I needed help physically while healing. I would not be able to do everything for myself. I would need assistance; in fact, it would be foolish of me not to ask for it. If I did not ask for physical help, I would put myself in danger of perhaps falling over walking up stairs or hurting my arm as I shut a car door. I would not view anyone physically rehabilitating as weak or dependent if they asked for help while healing.

◎ ◎ ◎ ◎ ◎

I will remember today that some of my emotional wounding has immobilised me just as physical wounding does. I know I will heal and what will help me heal is not pretending to do emotional tasks I am not strong enough to do yet. Pretending may actually hurt me and prolong healing time as I may do more damage.

◎ ◎ ◎ ◎ ◎

I am not weak if I ask for help. In fact it takes more courage and wisdom to ask for help with emotional wounding than it does for physical wounding.

◎ ◎ ◎ ◎ ◎

It is not up to me to decide whether others can or cannot help me. I will ask an adult to help me knowing that they can draw their own boundaries and say no. I will not ask a child to help me; adult emotional issues are too much for them. It is not a child's responsibility to take care of an adult.

◎ ◎ ◎ ◎ ◎

I may need professional help. I deserve the best help I can get. If it was my arm or leg that was damaged I would prefer that a professional helped me heal. My heart surely deserves the same respect.

◎ ◎ ◎ ◎ ◎

Asking for help is an act of courage. I choose to remember this today. These words are all I need to say:
When you have some time, could you please help me?

11. Letting go

The pain of leaving those you grow to love is only the
prelude to understanding yourself and others.

Shirley MacLaine

Joe and I separated on 27 November 1995 just five weeks after I put down drugs and alcohol. Our marriage did not work with me clean and sober. We were strangers.

Reality hit me hard at about three weeks without a drink or any drugs. I had also given up cigarettes so I was like a walking raw nerve. Reality was such a demanding place – the days seemed so long. I was exhausted by 8 p.m. and would need to go to bed.

Joe and I were invited to a friend's house for dinner. I did not want to go but with only five weeks' clean time up I did not yet know how to say no. I scoured my Barbie-like wardrobe for something to wear that covered me up. I did not want to be on show for the world. My new breasts now made me feel awkward; I just wanted to cover them up. I had cut my hair to shoulder length in an attempt to cut away the woman I was.

At the dinner party the music was loud and a joint was being passed around the table. I was constantly being coaxed to have a drink. I knew Joe was hoping I would loosen up and party with him again.

'Where's the party girl I married, just have a few drinks and a toke on the joint – you'll be fine', Joe whispered to me as I sat staring at the joint that had been passed to me. I looked at it long and hard. God, these people were boring. I had known them all for a decade or more, but had never socialised with them without drugs or alcohol. I did not want this life. I handed the joint on and excused myself and made my way to the bathroom.

I closed the toilet lid and sat on it with my head in my hands for a while. I just wanted to run away. As I looked out the window and saw the beautiful summer night's sky, the stars twinkled at me to remind me that they were there for me as they always had been.

'Show me how to do this, I don't know how to do this', I pleaded to my silver friends.

Joe was dancing to Van Morrison's 'Have I told you lately that I love you'. It was our song. He was waltzing around the room by himself and beckoned me to dance with him. The drugs and alcohol had kicked in and as he looked at me through glassy eyes I was overwhelmed with sadness. Such a beautiful man, a decent man, but I did not want to be with him any more, I did not really know who he was, and he had no idea that I was fighting for my life.

The next day I pleaded with him to stop using. He was sitting on a lounge chair after a long day at work. I knelt in front of him like you would beg a king on a throne for a pardon.

'Please stop partying for a while. I nearly picked up last night, it's too hard with you still using.' I looked at him desperately.

'Just because you have a problem, it doesn't mean that I have. I don't want to change my lifestyle, why should I?' he questioned defensively.

He was right. It was killing me but he was coping. He was comfortably numb.

'Because I will have to leave if you don't. I need to stay abstinent and I can't do that living like this.' I don't know where the words came from. I had not planned on saying that, and I had frightened myself in giving voice to my truth.

'Okay, off you go then', he dared me, standing up to indicate that he was terminating the conversation. He left the room. I was still on my knees in shock.

That night I slept on the couch, and cried until the sun came up. I knew I wanted to leave, but what about the boys? How would I tell them? How would I survive? Everything was in Joe's name; his mother made sure of that when we married. I had no income.

Joe had left for work early. I took the boys to school and then went straight to the Department of Social Security. It was such a hot day. I was wearing only a sarong and thongs. I had not bothered with any make-up; I knew I would just cry it off. My eyes were swollen and puffy from the previous night's lack of sleep. The queue was long. I was about twenty-fifth in the line. My pancreas was contracting. I had the electric fleas. It happens to people when they are detoxing. It feels like your skin is crawling with maggots. My body was in withdrawal from so many substances. I started to sob in the midst of the queue. I was too drained to be embarrassed.

'The lady in the pink sarong – room number four please', a woman from behind the counter beckoned me, waving her hand.

Everyone in the queue turned around to look at me.

'Over here, love', the woman gently called.

She opened the door to room four and ushered me in. I sat down and sobbed. I told her everything that had happened with Joe and me the night before, about my recovery attempt that was only five weeks old and about my beautiful boys.

'We need to get you out of there, love, and into a place of your own', she said placing her arm around my shoulder. She was a dolphin woman.

'I only have $70 in my purse, I can't afford a bond, I have no income', I could hardly focus, my tears seemed like they would never stop.

She took me to the Department of Housing and obtained an advance loan for my bond. She gave me a week's back pay of the single mother's pension and by that afternoon I had found a place only a few blocks away from my boys' school. It was a huge, old Queensland home that had been made into four flats. It was small but cosy.

I loaded everything I could into my Ford Laser and moved myself and the boys out.

I waited for Joe to beg me to come back. He knew I was broke and had no income. Maybe he just thought it was a matter of time before I returned. I sold my wedding rings and other things I could spare.

He did not know me. I would not go back. I had let go of a world I had trapped myself in. I was free. For the first time in my life I was the only one with a key to my home.

I managed the pension brilliantly and repaid my loan to the Department of Housing.

It was like jumping off the *Titanic* onto a flimsy life raft. Many said I was crazy for leaving the security of Ken and Barbie land. They thought I was losing my sanity.

In actual fact I was reclaiming it.

◎ Workout **11**

Letting go

I give myself permission to let go of relationships that consistently oppose me honouring my truth.

◎ ◎ ◎ ◎ ◎

In recovery, relationships that used to function because I would give my power away to the other person will not sustain themselves once I commence to reclaim my power.

◎ ◎ ◎ ◎ ◎

I will remember that if I choose change it does not make me superior to or better than the other person – just different.

◎ ◎ ◎ ◎ ◎

Children will learn the most valuable lessons from watching adults who live peaceful lives of self-respect and consistency, derived from choice not obligation. If I am living in an emotional war zone or having a relationship that involves emotional neglect, denial and criticism, this is what any child watching will believe is acceptable.

◎ ◎ ◎ ◎ ◎

Whenever I let go of a relationship it is of the utmost importance that I hold onto my truth, that I don't self-abandon, that I hold the hand of that small child inside of me with reassurance that they deserve to be treated with love and dignity.

◎ ◎ ◎ ◎ ◎

Sometimes letting go of friends and children as they move away is also difficult. I will remember today that people are free spirits; it is a privilege to be included in another's life, not a right. If I have been a safe loving person to the one leaving, our hearts will always be connected no matter where they are on the planet.

◎ ◎ ◎ ◎ ◎

Today, if I need to let go of a relationship, either personal or professional, I will remember:
I deserve to be treated with respect and dignity … I am responsible for the choices I have made to date … I am not responsible for another's happiness … I am allowed to choose who I have relationships with … Obligation always leads to resentment.

12. Oh, to just feel good enough

Change occurs when one becomes who they are, not when
they try to become who they are not.

Ruth P Freedman

Filling in my days was a challenge. I spent a great deal of time sunbaking at public swimming pools. One day I overheard two women as they sat in the summer sun at the Newmarket pool cooing about an amazing swimmer. They said he showed up at Centenary swimming pool at 9 a.m. every morning.

'He's a chef – I have spoken to him – and my God, what a swimmer. He used to play water polo for Australia. He's a treat to watch', one of the women said with delight as she straightened her towel.

Ah, ha! That's what I'll do, I'll go and watch this man swim. I had nothing else to do with my mornings. I had to learn how to fill in my days without all my 'Absolutely Fabulous' Patsy and Edwina-style girlfriends. I was now a bore to them.

'What's on my sandwiches, Mum?' Sam asked as he pulled his backpack up over his shoulders.

'Ham and cheese, and I also put in a special little treat!'

'Yummm', he smiled and cheekily licked his lips.

The boys were down the stairs and hopping into the car ready for Monday morning at school. My stomach was full of butterflies. I was anxious and excited as I checked myself in the mirror. I bent over and cupped my breasts in my hands to lift them up higher in my bikini top. A bit more jiggling and I had them sitting with perfect cleavage. I could use some of that tape models use to hold them still – if only they would sit like that all day. I felt silly. He probably wouldn't even be there, but if he were, would I be able to pick him out from all the other morning swimmers? This woman I had eavesdropped on had said that he was the fastest swimmer by far, so he should be easy to spot.

I tucked my hair behind my ears, put on a touch of barely there lipstick, rubbed my lips together and looked into my own eyes one more time.

'My God, am I desperate or what? Why am I even doing this? I am stalking a man I have never met before!' I had nothing else to do with my morning other than sit around and contemplate my navel. It would do me good to sit in the sun anyway. I was convinced. I grabbed the keys and pulled the door shut.

There were so many people at the pool at this ungodly hour, 8.30 a.m. Being a person who had never exercised and had grown up in a family who did no exercise it was like entering a whole new world. I paid my entrance fee and stood near the kiosk as I surveyed the best place to spy. Every lane of the Olympic-sized pool was filled with swimmers. As my eyes glanced across the pool I saw him immediately, or rather felt him. His stroke was powerful, his body was long, his hair from what I could see was black – shame, I favoured blondes – and the way he swam was like a dolphin. His upper torso was moving through the water like a machine churning the water from beneath him with perfect rhythm. I stood there totally blank and just watched him for a few minutes. What would it be like to be that free and strong in the water, I wondered.

I was not a strong swimmer; in actual fact I could not put my face in the water and swim at all. Some of my childhood abuse had occurred with my father in water while learning to water-ski on the Murray River. I could dog paddle and back or side stroke but that was it. My face had to be out of the water.

'Can I help you?' the girl at the kiosk asked.

She startled me; I was standing right next to the counter in a daze.

'Just a bottle of water, thanks', I answered counting out the 20-cent pieces in my purse. It was the first time in years I had to watch what I spent. Joe had always been generous with housekeeping money; in fact, I had handled all the bills and juggled the money as I chose. There was always enough for extras, but not now, not on a pension. I didn't mind, I honestly preferred things this way. Joe was still angry with me and would not help me financially at all, and I did not ask. I had left all the furniture with him – I wanted nothing that reminded me of the violence, the arguments, the drugs and the sex. It all seemed like someone else's life now. Cindy's life, not Cynthia's life, I decided.

From this moment onward I would now only use my full name. I had always loved it but it felt too good for me, as though I was not elegant or special enough to be called Cynthia. My name meant 'Goddess of Mount Cynthus'. It was an old Greek derivative, I had read somewhere, and Cynthia also meant 'Moon Goddess', for Mount Cynthus was where people in ancient times used to sit and contemplate the awesome beauty of the moon. I was starting a new life – a life that was no longer edited or a pretence, a wholesome life that deserved my whole name.

'That will be $1.10, thanks', the girl behind the kiosk said impatiently as I wandered off into thought about my name, forgetting she was waiting for me.

'Sorry, I've got it. Do you mind a few 5-cent pieces?' I asked, counting them into her hand.

'That's fine', she lied, impatience written all over her face.

I felt inadequate, like a fraud for even being in such a healthy place as this. Could they tell I did not belong here, I wondered.

I sucked in my stomach, pulled my shoulders back and made my way over to the stands closest to his lane. The stands were big concrete steps wide enough to lie on, so I spread out my purple beach sheet making sure that there were no creases and sat down. My hat had a huge brim so I could look out from under it without being conspicuous. His swimming was truly beautiful to watch. It was like a meditation. I felt peaceful as I watched him swim up, tumble turn, and then go back. Every now and then he would stop and check the clock, have a sip from his drink bottle and then start again. The sound of the water splashing was so relaxing. An hour passed and the morning sun was getting hot on my back. I wanted to get into the pool but felt too self-conscious. I did not want him to notice me, or know I was watching. It was giving me such inexplicable pleasure that I decided to wait until he had left to get in.

He climbed the steps at the side of the pool. As his body emerged from the water I could see he was a very tall man. His hair was long, shoulder length, and black. His skin was very tanned and smooth, and he was not hairy, which I was pleased about.

Weeks passed before I eventually got up courage to get into the water while he was still in the pool.

Now was my chance – the lane next to him was empty. I had hired a kickboard from the kiosk, a little yellow surfboard-like thing that I had watched other women hold to their chest as they kicked with their back in the water. Face out of the water, kicking – I could do that.

As I have mentioned, I am a chameleon, a mimic, and had been all my life. I always believed that other women were better than me. I always felt less than them.

So I had watched these female swimmers with great attention over the previous weeks. I had watched how they bent their arm over their head, touching their opposite shoulder and pausing as they stretched, and how they grabbed their foot and bent their leg behind them while standing on one foot, pausing again to stretch and then repeating it with the other leg. I could do that. The goggles and the swimming cap were not an attractive look – I decided they had to go. As for the one-piece Speedos, well my crochet leather string bikini was a little more interesting I decided. A bit of waterproof mascara, a touch of barely there lipstick, as I dug into my string beach bag and grabbed my brush quickly, raking it through my shoulder-length mousy brown hair. Breasts in place – check; bikini line clean – check; hair right – check; don't forget the kickboard – check; here I go.

He was halfway down the pool as I sat on the edge, dangling my feet in the water. Oops, forgot to do my stretches! I stood up and did the arm and leg stuff quite convincingly, I thought, pausing with the right facial expressions. I was impressed. He had turned and was heading back towards me. Now was the time to do it. Would I get in now, or wait until he turned, because sometimes he stopped and had a sip from his drink bottle? The butterflies increased with each stroke he took. Nope, couldn't get in yet. I waited for him to turn, looking preoccupied with my bikini strap and ignoring him as his huge feet splashed me as they surfaced like a whale turning only centimetres away. I was so nervous. I had never courted a man in my life without the aid of alcohol or drugs. The thought of having sex with a man without alcohol as an anaesthetic made me panic. But this man was drawing me to him like a magnet.

He was way down the other end so I got in. I held the little yellow foam board to my breasts and stretched out. I didn't have to kick very hard to move myself through the water. Ah, it was lovely. It was like a stroll lying down. The blue sky was just glorious – I could have been on a Greek island somewhere. I decided to do this every day whether he was there or not. He would pass me from time to time and I could feel his energy as the wash of his huge body made me lose my rhythm. I hit the plastic lane ropes quite a bit; I could not work out how to go in a straight line. I was aware I was zigzagging; I hoped no-one had noticed. I had done perhaps ten laps when I felt someone tap the top of my head.

'I just can't watch you hit your head again', he said with genuine concern.

I stood up and I know my face was red with embarrassment. I had been hitting my head on the pool wall because I had no idea that the changing colour of the floating lane ropes helped you know that you were getting close to the end. I did not have an aquatic bone in my body.

'My name's Brad, Brad Morton', he smiled.

He pulled his goggles off to reveal the most beautiful eyes I had ever seen. His eyelashes were wet and very long, his eyes a soft blue framed by very dark eyebrows. I was staring; he was staring back at me and smiling. God, I wondered who lived inside those eyes. They were like an entrance to a special world I had hoped existed all my life. It was as though his pupils were a gateway to an enchanted forest that was his soul; it was lush and green, mysterious and sacred. His eyes were safe; they felt like home. I had known this feeling before when I looked into my Papa's eyes as a little girl. I knew I needed to say something quickly, but I felt awkward. It was blatantly obvious that I in my crochet leather string bikini zigzagging up and down the pool banging my head on the end wall did not have a clue what I was doing.

That summed up how I felt about life.

◎ Workout 12

Oh, to just feel good enough

Every time I tell myself I am not good enough, I self-abandon.
I tell myself that who I am and what I stand for is wrong or less
than what other people stand for. It is vanity turned inside out.
There is nothing humble about a self-defeating attitude.

It is also self-obsessive for me to believe that everyone else is
like me and judges my worth on how I look. Dolphin people
are more interested in who I am than what I am.

I will only feel not good enough today if I compare myself
with another and then decide that I am less than they are.

I will remember that I am a human being, not a performing
seal. The only person I really require respect from is myself. If I
can bear the accusation of betrayal and not betray my own
soul I will then build trust and a sense of loyalty to myself.
Only when I can trust myself and be loyal to myself can I truly
be that with another.

What others do for a living, look like, drive or earn is none of
my business. I will focus on minding my own business in my
head and heart and will find that peace results. When I focus
on others, I lose sight of myself. When I lose myself, life loses
meaning.

Telling myself I am not good enough is harvesting shame. If I
feel ashamed because I believe I am less than others, I am
disempowering myself. I give power to whomever I perceive is
better than me.

What will sustain me from the inside today is being honest about who I am and who I am not. I choose not to give my power away today by pretending.

I choose to remember I am good enough today because:
Who I am and what I am is all I have to give today and quite simply that is good enough.

13. Grieving for the perfect family fairytale

It is difficult to define grief and joy. Each is finite. Each will fade.

Jim Bishop

My papa – my grandfather – saved my heart as a little girl. He was the one person with whom I felt safe. We would go to Glenelg beach in Adelaide alone, just him and me. In the early Sixties there were trampolines and a mini sideshow on the beachfront. He would patiently stand at the side of the trampoline longer than anyone else's parents. And he would watch me and smile. With every trick I did he would throw his head back and raise his eyebrows in delight. If I wanted more time, he would just pay the man. I brought him joy and he showed that so honestly to me.

Papa and I did not speak a lot, but we held hands as we spent hours walking down by the water's edge. He smoked a pipe that smelled wonderful. He would fill it full of Old Port tobacco. I loved watching the ritual and the sound of the end of the pipe as it clicked his teeth. He was like Popeye, but funnier.

I was always sad to leave him. I remember not wanting to wash my hands after a visit with him. The beautiful aroma of Old Port tobacco lingered in my palms from holding his hands. I would stare out the car window as I was driven away from him, cupping my small hands over my nose, closing my eyes and inhaling the love that was my papa.

I had been dating Brad for a few months. He was a true gentleman. He also liked to just look at me and smile. I brought him joy I know because his eyes told the truth, like Papa's.

Things were not going well with the remainder of my family. The more time that passed with me being clean and sober, the more friction and discomfort seemed to grow between us all. Any time I saw them, I left wanting a drink or drugs. I did not connect with these people, they were strangers. I also really wanted to be called by my full name.

'I don't want to call you Cynthia, you're Cindy to me' was often the response.

They did not like the changes in me. It seemed the more of myself I reclaimed the less of me they accepted. I so wanted to be perfect, to not be a problem to them. But the harder I worked on my recovery and speaking my truth, the deeper the rift became.

I had my first sober Christmas at my sister's house. It was horrific. It was the first Christmas that the boys and I spent as a broken family. All of our hearts were sad. My mother and I used to get drunk every Christmas and my sister would panic and with clenched jaw pretend that she enjoyed our company. None of us really got along, but we all pretended we did. And we had the fairytale photos to comfort us that at least we looked 'normal'.

My grandmother, who had also survived incest as a child, was at my sister's house that Christmas, criticising and questioning everyone around her with her acid tongue.

'I think Cindy is having a nervous breakdown', she said to my mother as I sat outside alone crying. They had both followed me, as they were drawn to wounding like moths to a flame. They spoke to each other as if I could not hear them.

'What's wrong with her, Joan?' My grandmother spat the words at my mother expecting a quick explanation.

I had heard that phrase from my grandmother's mouth many times over the years: 'What's wrong with her, Joan? She needs a tonic, she's too thin.' I had heard those words from as far back as I could remember.

'She has horrible thin hair like us, Joan, it looks like string. Cindy, you're lucky your mother is a hairdresser, you know a woman's hair is her crowning glory.'

Criticism was the only language my grandmother knew. I must have reminded her of herself. I wrote the poem opposite after that Christmas day, knowing it would be the last I would spend with my biological family. Papa would understand.

The Cactus

Her words are like invisible splinters naked to the eye
I have to stay at her house – I'd really rather die
She picks at my weakness like a vulture circling waiting for death
I hide under Papa's bed, as she walks past I hold my breath

Her hands are sharp, they snatch and they slap
The only safe refuge is on beautiful Papa's lap
Her voice is like vinegar, I block my ears to stop the sound
She is nasty and mean to me especially when no-one else is around

Why does she hate me? Because I am just like her
Old childhood wounding my presence does stir
The family trail … the apple never falls very far from the tree
We both have known incest and her old memories won't let her be

She spits that I need a tonic; I am not right and way too thin
Terrible hair, not very smart, but I might get good skin
Her home is full of ornaments but no friends ever drop by
But Papa loves her, his eyes smile; he is there when she needs to cry

Her skinny hair, tight lips curled in regret
Sad eyes, angry heart – if only she could make herself forget
She died without healing, rocking in her bed
I chose not to see her; some things are better left unsaid

Dearest Grandma I now understand you too were alone
A prisoner held captive in a clean and proper home
Thank you cactus, my grandma, for messages so clear
I'll break this cycle, heal my wounds and no longer live in fear

Your life was a gift to me of what not to do
You were a teacher, albeit harsh, your message really got through
Your grandchildren are brave; they can love and are free
No more secrets or unspoken anger – everything was meant to be.

I got news that Papa was unwell in late May 1996. Brad and I had become a couple and I had finally introduced him to Sam and Mitchell. They thought he was cool because he would play Lego with them for hours.

I drove down to the Gold Coast where Papa was in hospital. Brad minded the boys for me. Things were strained between me, Mum and Georgie, my sister. We had not spoken much over the past months. We were all comfortable it seemed with silence as we gathered in the hospital foyer.

I had some time alone with Papa. We just held hands. He said so much with his eyes and his touch. Like Brad did. I had thought that my Papa would be the only male that would ever know how to do that with me.

'I love you, Papa', I choked with tears as I leaned over and kissed his heavily stubbled cheek.

He said nothing, but his eyes told me he knew I was leaving the family and that it was probably a good thing for me. He loved me no matter what. I left before the others and cried all the way home listening to ballads from Guns and Roses. My heart felt like it was going to break with grief for my beautiful papa; I knew I would not see him again. I had just said my final goodbye.

It was the eve of 6 June that I received the news that Papa's condition was critical. I huddled up in my flannelette pyjamas and climbed into bed. I had given Brad a key to my unit. When he finished cooking at the restaurant late at night he would come and visit me. I loved the sound of his key in the door. It was like Father Christmas coming. I became so excited just being in his presence.

Brad's warm body holding me that night brought me to tears. As he kissed my face, his heavy stubble comforted me. His love was so strong yet gentle like Papa's. As the night hours passed I was suddenly awoken, hit by a huge wave of grief – I felt Papa die. It was as though his energy came to me in the night and he said goodbye. It seemed that he was passing a baton on to Brad. It was safe for him to leave now that I had a new dolphin male to take his place. He was tired and wanted to go.

I realised the relevance of the date the following morning. It was 7 June, Brad's birthday. Papa died on the day Brad was born.

As the grief has faded over time the sacred colour of Papa's love has become clearer and more beautiful with each passing year.

I often wondered what it would be like to grow up in a family like The Waltons where everyone brings out the best in each other, and no matter what happens the parents always remain emotionally available to their children.

It only takes one person to sew the seeds of love in a child's life. I am so grateful I had my Papa – he did that for me.

I have come to understand that the perfect family fairytale is rare.

◎ Workout 13

Grieving for the perfect family fairytale

Grief is one of the hardest emotions to sit with. It is deep and overwhelming. Like a tidal wave out of nowhere it can knock you off your emotional feet and convince you that you are going to drown in it. The only way to survive grief is to surrender to it, to roll with it and not fight it, and eventually to come to the surface again. And with each wave you survive, you become emotionally fitter – you learn grief is a process you cannot control. Grief does fade over time. It becomes less overwhelming. It transforms into a gentle sadness that has a beauty to it.

◎ ◎ ◎ ◎ ◎

Being afraid of grief is what makes it so difficult to process. It is helpful for me to make contact with a dolphin person if I feel grief rising within myself. Holding someone's hand as I cry or rock myself will help me stay in the here and now and not be swallowed up by yesterday or tomorrow. Projecting about the future while in the midst of a wave of grief is like putting on concrete boots. It just makes the grief harder to endure.

◎ ◎ ◎ ◎ ◎

Grief is sometimes dismissed as self-pity. It does such damage to a human heart to not validate its pain. It's like dismissing a gun wound as nothing to be concerned about. Emotion ignored becomes infected, creating more pain. Unacknowledged grief can have dire effects on a human heart.

Grief is a natural emotion. It is the heart's way of detoxing pain. To understand grief and to honour its process is essential for emotional fitness.

I will honour grief today and remember:
Mother Nature has more faith in me than I have in myself ... She knows I am stronger than I give myself credit for... If grief arises in my life today I will remember that I can survive it if I don't fight it ... It too shall pass.

14. What is love?

The story of a love is not important –
What is important is that one is capable of love.
It is perhaps the only glimpse we are permitted of eternity.

Helen Hayes

Brad and I had been living together for only a few months, and for the first time in my life I was beginning to really trust a male partner with my heart. It was scary. I was in uncharted emotional waters.

He was truly a dolphin male. His actions spoke of who he was, not just his words. I could also trust his words because his actions aligned with them. For example, he would say that he wanted to put a vegetable garden in the backyard, and lo and behold the following Saturday morning at 6 a.m. a truck would be delivering topsoil to the backyard for the new garden. And he would spend hours creating it. He would also promise to take the dog for a walk or hang the washing out when the football game had finished. And he would actually follow through and do it. So I was beginning to trust what he said, because he would do what he said. I felt safe with him. I had been used to men who said a lot of pretty things, but when push came to shove, they never backed it up with action. They were not there for me, and I know it was partially because I was not there for them either. It was an endless cycle. Perhaps I had attracted this man because I was ready for change.

I was beginning to know in my heart that I really loved him, and that made me hate him for making me so vulnerable. I had successfully protected my heart from vulnerability for decades and now he had somehow got in under my radar.

We had just had a wonderful Sunday together doing not much. We had slept in, and had then gone and had lunch at 'The Brekky Creek', which is a famous pub in my hometown that serves wonderful steaks in an outdoor Spanish garden.

I wanted him to look at me and tell me he loved me. I loved the sound of his voice. When he looked at me it was as though his eyes were his hands – they would touch me and turn on what felt like tiny coloured Christmas tree lights inside my soul.

I had grown up with domestic violence but did not know it until after this particular day.

Abuse in my home was called discipline and my father's violence was a result of him caring about us, we were told.

I remember being knocked off my chair at the dinner table at five years of age because a pea spilled off my plate or because I looked at my father the wrong way. He would stand over me and make me eat carrots that I had vomited up onto my plate, and hit me across the head until I ate them.

When he was angry it was like he was in a trance and no-one could reach him. Often the next day he would be remorseful. He would never say sorry, because we were always told that violence was good for us, that we needed manners, and that he hit us because he cared about how we would turn out. Dad would often bring a special chocolate or cream bun home from work for us the day after one of these outbursts. He would ruffle my hair as he walked past me and call me 'Suzie'. I don't know where that name came from but I liked it. He could never say he loved me, but when he said 'How's my Suzie' I knew that was what he was trying to say. His hands spoke. When he was not violent his beautiful tanned hands with square nails gave off love. As he ruffled my hair I closed my eyes with delight at his gentle touch.

So I came to understand that there was a pattern. Males were violent first, but always showed love afterwards. So violence for me was a part of love. It was how love was delivered.

I recall sitting in class at school pressing on the bruises on my thighs, enjoying the distraction of the gentle pain that came from putting pressure on the bruises. The physical distraction was easier to cope with than my emotional reality. I would think to myself 'My dad really loves me' as I pressed down on my purpled thighs. It was a comfort. My love as a child came packaged with violence.

It was no different with male partners I chose later in life. If they were not violent it meant they did not care. However, if a man hit me, it meant that I mattered to him. And the cycle continued. If I wanted to hear a male say they loved me I would start a fight. I became adept at using what I call 'the verbal knife'. One slash and I could get a reaction. When I was in shark mode, I knew how to bring out their shark. I would verbally attack their mother, their untidiness around the house or their mates. I would always get a reaction.

If they did not react I would increase the stab wounds with my verbal knife, and on the odd occasion that they would walk away or try to retreat, I would become physically violent with them. I always chose men bigger than me; I figured it had to be a fair fight. I would throw something at them or punch or hit them. They would defend themselves, we would physically fight, and of course I always lost. The next day they would have a battered woman on their hands and the remorse part of the cycle would kick in. I would get flowers and would be told I was loved. Mission accomplished.

So on this tranquil Sunday afternoon I was hungry to hear Brad, my new dolphin man, tell me he loved me. So of course I did my usual thing – I got out the verbal knife.

'Would you mind not leaving your boots where you decide to take them off?' I bitched as I let out a heavy martyred sigh and picked them up.

'Cynthia, what's up?' He asked with a gentle concerned tone. 'We have had such a lovely afternoon together, why the sudden change? What's the matter?'

Hmmm, not quite the response I was looking for. He was far too rational for me. Obviously I would have to use the verbal knife again.

'Are you going to just watch television all afternoon now?' I questioned, placing my hands on my hips and ignoring his plea for an explanation.

'Cynthia, why are you being such a bitch? This is becoming a pattern with you. What's the time, let's see?' he asked, looking at his watch. 'Yep, it's 4 o'clock – it was about this time last Sunday when you tried to start a fight. Why do you want to spoil the day?' he asked still in a rational and caring tone.

This guy just did not get it. How was I going to upset him so he would tell me he loved me? Well, I will have to get the ball rolling, I thought to myself. Brad was no wimp. He stood 191 centimetres tall and used to play water polo for Australia. He was a fit and strong man and a lot bigger than me. I decided that I would push him around a little to let him know I really wanted to fight. I leaned forward and poked him in the chest to show him that I was angry.

'Hey, now listen', he said, backing away from me and holding his hands up in a surrender motion. 'I have no desire to be in a relationship with a violent woman. If you ever touch me again while you're angry, I'm gone and I won't be back. If I ever touch you when I am angry you need to leave me because people who love each other don't hit each other.'

I was dumbfounded. I was 34 years of age and had never heard that before from a male. My heart heard it though, loud and clear. I knew he meant it – I could trust that his words would be followed up with action.

I went to my shrink the next day and recounted the events of the Sunday afternoon.

'I don't think this guy really loves me, I think he's a bit soft', I whispered to my shrink.

'No, no', my shrink assured me. 'Cynthia, this man is the first man who has ever really loved you.'

A tear rolled down my cheek. I knew it was the truth.

◎ Workout 14

What is love for me today?

Can I truly say to myself today that I love myself or another? Do I know what love means to me today? Love can be described as choosing to want only the best for another, to have unconditional love. What does that mean to me? Does it exist? If I have unconditional love for another does that mean letting go of my own moral code for them? And if I don't let go of my personal values, does that mean my love is conditional?

◎ ◎ ◎ ◎ ◎

Maybe true love to me is conditional upon my own self-preservation. For if I don't preserve who I am and what I stand for in life, who will? Would true love returned ask me to let go of my values and moral code for love or go against my primal instincts of self-preservation?

◎ ◎ ◎ ◎ ◎

Would I lie, cheat or steal if a loved one asked me to? Would I betray myself in order not to betray them? Is my sense of self and love for myself healthy enough to preserve my dignity and not look for the approval of the one I love at the expense of my personal integrity?

◎ ◎ ◎ ◎ ◎

Is true love about hope and preference but without obligation and expectation? If another needs to have me meet their needs, maybe they are not taking good enough care of themselves and their own needs? Do I want to be a caretaker or a lover? Can I separate love and need? Is love to me about choice, patience and freedom of my spirit, celebration, gratitude, dreams, beauty and joy?

◎ ◎ ◎ ◎ ◎

What love is *not* may be the best way for me to work out what love is for me today:
Love is not control, ownership, violent, needy, a drug, expectation, pretence, dictatorial, a trophy, money, sex or able to be turned on and off at a whim – it is not about losing me, but about being me.

15. Coping with remorse

Our feelings are our most genuine paths to knowledge.

Audre Lorde

It was Thursday night, my favourite television night because 'E.R.' was on. Dinner was over and done with, the boys were doing the dishes, Brad was still at work, so the television was all mine. I had my oversized, faded pink flannelette pyjamas on with matching pink bed socks and was in comfort heaven. Why the world did not do business in pyjamas baffled me. They have always been the most comfortable way to dress as far as I am concerned. I had the cushions at just the right angle under my head as the 'E.R.' music started up.

It was about halfway through the episode and the tension was building when all of a sudden I heard a thud on the wall of the next room. I ignored it, annoyed that the noise had made me miss a few important words of dialogue.

Thud, thud, bang! Only a few seconds had passed and I heard it again. I went cold inside. They were the noises of a body being slammed up against a wall. That sound brought back a flood of memories from my childhood.

I remembered being about twelve years of age, so my sister, Georgie, would have been about fourteen and my baby brother, Adam, four. I would be wakened in the dead of night by that same sound – thud, thud, bang. My father would be drunk and my mother hysterical. Some nights we lay in bed frozen in fear; other nights we got up and tried to rescue Mum. Both options made us feel powerless. He was too angry and too strong.

Bang, bang, thud, bang, thud, thud – it was getting worse. I flew off the couch and out into the living room where my two boys were fighting.

My youngest boy, Mitchell, was like a raging bull. His nostrils were flared and his eyes blinded by rage. I knew that face, I saw my father. He was lunging for his brother when I stood in between them. I grabbed Mitchell by the shoulders and dug my fingernails deep into his flesh. I pushed him backward. I screamed at him. I don't even recall what I said.

I just roared back at him, summoning all the rage I had saved up for my father. I was so scared of my own son. My reflex response was to try and scare him even more. At that moment I hated all men – I hated that they could scare me and overpower me. And all those years of venom came spewing out of my mouth at my child. He looked back at me with eyes full of rage. I felt sure he wanted to hit me. My heart was pounding, my breathing heavy as if I had just run a race. He stormed to his bedroom and slammed the door behind him so hard that a picture fell off the wall onto the floor and the glass broke.

I was numb.

I went back to the television room and resumed watching 'E.R.' as if nothing had happened. I could not speak; it was as though I was in a trance.

Brad came home about twenty minutes later and could feel the tension hanging in the air as he walked down the hallway. The house was in silence. I had turned off the television and was staring at the grey screen.

'What happened?' he said knowingly. Maybe it was the look on my face or the unusual silence of the house at that time of night, but he knew something was wrong.

I went out and sat in the lounge room with him and recounted the evening's events. I started to sob. I told him how I was so ashamed of how I had unleashed all of my rage onto Mitchell.

'You never solve violence with violence', he assured me gently as he rubbed my knee. 'You need to talk to Mitchell and explain what you just did to me, to him. He's just a kid – my dad taught me so much and I respect him because he was never violent with me', he said with admiration in his eyes as he spoke of his father.

'Mitchell, could you come into the lounge room, I need to talk to you', I asked sheepishly as I opened his bedroom door.

He was still very angry with me, and very hurt. He walked slowly into the room and unwillingly plonked himself down in the big armchair. He would not look at me. I knelt in front of him with my hands on his knees.

'Please look at me Mitch.' He continued to look away. There was silence. I closed my eyes and remembered my extra mile checkpoints.

I knew that I had to make this apology without an emotional investment in the outcome. He may still need to remain angry for a while. I could not force him to look at me. I had already imposed myself on him enough for one night.

Yes, he and his brother had been fighting and that needed to be sorted out later, but that's a part of life for brothers. I was the adult and I had lost it. For my self-respect, I needed to apologise.

'I am so sorry.' The words got stuck in my throat and I knew I was going to cry.

'Mitchell, I am so very sorry for hurting your arms and for unloading all of the pain that belongs with my dad onto you.' I was sobbing now.

'You just frightened me, and when I get afraid I get angry at whoever I think has made me afraid. I was scared of your anger because I couldn't separate you from my dad. You became my dad, and that is my stuff. I need to talk to Mal about it in my next session. It's not your fault', I explained.

'Sweetheart, I am so, so sorry. Mitchy, please forgive me', I pleaded, putting my head on his knees and letting years of tears come flooding out.

'It's all right Mum, I am sorry too. I didn't mean to scare you.' He leant down and hugged me. We cried together.

◎ Workout **15**

Coping with remorse

I feel remorse when I have violated one of my own moral codes. For example, most people feel remorse if they hit a child in an act of rage for they have violated their own moral code and hurt themselves. Remorse is the appropriate emotion to accompany an act like this.

◎ ◎ ◎ ◎ ◎

This feeling of remorse is a wonderful alarm system and a very uncomfortable emotion to remind me not to take such action again.

◎ ◎ ◎ ◎ ◎

The only way to relieve myself of remorse is to be responsible for my actions, to own them, to blame no other and to make amends to the person or persons I have wounded without the expectation that they will bounce back immediately. I then need not to beat myself up, but to learn from and be grateful for the discomfort of remorse, and not to repeat the behaviour.

◎ ◎ ◎ ◎ ◎

Words to listen for that accompany coping responsibly with remorse:

I am sorry ... I was wrong ... Please forgive me ... Would you like me to leave you be?... What can I do for you?... I will do my best not to ever do that again.

16. Personal boundaries

Don't compromise yourself.
You are all you've got.

Janis Joplin

I was not used to emotional equality in any relationship. In the past it had always been about whose turn it was to give. One person was dominant, the other submissive.

Giving was only ever done to receive. If I wanted a partner to go to a function they did not want to go to I always pulled out some ammunition from the past. 'Well, I really didn't want to go to your mother's for dinner last week, but I went, for you. I don't think it's too much to ask that you come to this with me.'

I had attracted men who knew how to play the emotional scoreboard – there is no giving unless it buys you permission to recall the debt when it suits you.

Brad did not play this game.

He was a man's man. He did not style his hair or care if the wallet in his pocket spoiled the shape of his bottom. He was who he was no matter who was in the room. His personality did not change for anyone. There were two sorts of people in the world as far as he was concerned: people who were straight shooters and dickheads. He did not care what people did for a living, what they drove or what they looked like. If you were insincere he would not give you the time of day. I admired that about him. He was not scared of people or of being unpopular. That made him attractive to me.

I became confused as to why this man was with me. He was a chef in an award-winning restaurant. He could cook far better than I could. He was used to doing his own laundry and did not like me to iron his clothes.

'I don't feel a need to iron your shirts, I'll iron my own. It's not your job to do it', he said as I stood gobsmacked that he did not see caring for his clothes as a woman's job.

I certainly was no sex goddess in the bedroom. I was more like a timid lamb that took a long time to relax and surrender to his touch. I was confused. All of the roles that I had been programmed to believe as a child growing up in Ken and Barbie land were a woman's job this man was not interested in. He didn't need me to cook, wash and iron his clothes, or perform like a whore in bed.

'Why are you with me, if you don't want me to cook, clean and give you heaps of sex?' I naively asked him with sincere confusion.

'Because of who you are', he reassured me.

It took quite some time for me to stop trying to control and manipulate him. I was used to men having me purchase their clothes and tell them what to wear before we went out.

One Sunday morning we were going out for breakfast. I had spent the past hour getting my hair and clothes perfect for what was to be a relaxed late brunch.

I walked into the bedroom to see Brad pulling on a pair of jeans that had been on the floor all night. The shirt he was wearing was not one of my favourites. I did not like the fabric – it was old-fashioned. His jeans were very crumpled.

'You're not wearing those out today are you?' I questioned condescendingly.

'Yes, Cynthia, I am. I would not insult you by telling you what to wear, so don't insult me by telling me', he said firmly as he did up his fly.

'I can give them a quick iron for you if you like; it's just that they're really crushed', I said defensively.

'Cynthia I want a woman in my life, not a mother, just back off, okay?'

My ego was bruised, but my heart was relieved. I had always been bored by men who looked to me for guidance and reassurance. I felt like I was dressing three children when I had to leave the house, instead of two.

This man knew the boundary of where I finished and where he began.

A few years later my oldest son, Sam, was going to meet a new girlfriend's parents for the first time. They were society people and I was also meeting them as I was the designated chauffeur on the date.

'Sam, don't you think a collared shirt might be a better idea than a T-shirt. You're meeting her parents for the first time', I said, concerned that he did not look his best.

'Mum, I wear T-shirts, it's who I am; if they don't like it, well it's just bad luck. I am not going to change what I like to wear for any girl or her parents', he said respectfully but firmly.

My children were far wiser than I had ever been at their age. Years of living with Brad had paid off. The boys had learnt from watching him that they did not have to change themselves for anyone, not even me, their mother.

They felt safe enough to assert their boundaries with me. I felt like I was getting some things right.

◎ Workout 16

Personal boundaries

The most important person for me to respect today is myself. I do this when I self-preserve and don't allow others to trample my personal boundaries. If I do not assert my boundaries and respect myself, I cannot ask others for what I am not willing to give myself.

◎ ◎ ◎ ◎ ◎

I teach others how to treat me by the way I conduct my relationship with myself.

◎ ◎ ◎ ◎ ◎

Do I treat myself as well as I treat those I love? Do I always give myself the burnt chop? Do I honestly believe I am as worthy as others? Do I allow myself to be dominated, controlled or abused, or taken for granted? If so, it is my responsibility to make changes if I am unhappy. I am not powerless unless I believe I am.

◎ ◎ ◎ ◎ ◎

I realise today that the relationship I am having with myself is mirrored in the relationships I have with others in my personal and public life.

◎ ◎ ◎ ◎ ◎

I respect others who don't allow me to dominate them. I feel safe with people who know where they finish and I begin. I don't like others invading my emotional boundaries, so I will not do that to others today.

◎ ◎ ◎ ◎ ◎

I can self-preserve and retain healthy personal boundaries for myself today by:

- caring for myself with healthy meals, sleep and laughter
- remembering that I can say 'no'
- remembering that I am good enough, and that it is my responsibility to look after my own needs.

17. Being vulnerable

Our children need to know that we are not perfect, and it's better if they hear it from us.

Anne Wilson Schaef

Writing has never been a problem with my dyslexia, but reading what I have written back is a huge problem – and comprehension is where my dyslexia is rampant. The words get tangled in my mind and putting what I have written in context is extremely difficult.

It was April 2000 and I had finally finished the draft of my first book. I was so full of doubt that the book didn't make any sense to me at all.

My oldest son, Sam, had been the dux of his school and was brilliant at English. My youngest boy, Mitchell, was also very bright but I felt a little too young to fully understand what I was trying to say in that book.

'Sam, would you be comfortable editing my manuscript and marking any areas that don't make sense?' I asked as he lay sprawled on his bed reading a *Mad* magazine. His floor was littered with clothes, clean and dirty. I tried to ignore the mess. He was in his element munching on chocolate and swigging cold milk from a glass as he read.

'Sure, just leave it on my table. Can I just do it when I feel like it, and not right now?' he checked cautiously.

'Yep, just when you get a chance – I'm not in a hurry. Are you sure you feel comfortable about it?', I asked again, knowing how he hates it when I repeat myself. I was really trying to assure myself that I felt comfortable exposing my truth to my son. I felt so vulnerable being honest. I had flaunted all of my flaws in this book in order to help understand myself. Was it going to be too confronting for him to read about all his mother's imperfections in black and white? Would he lose respect for me if he knew everything about me? These were my major concerns.

'Yeah, why wouldn't I?' he answered in his invincible teenage tone.

I balanced it on his crammed bedside table, picking up the freshly drained glass of milk. I had done it, not only bared my soul to my child but asked him for constructive criticism. I navigated my way around the dirty clothes and shut the door behind me.

Two weeks passed and the book was still on his bedside table. It was all I could do not to ask him if he had read any of it yet. But I had told him he could take his time, and I knew if I nagged him, it would become a chore to him and I certainly didn't want that.

During the third week I was downstairs hanging out the last of five loads of washing. It was around 6 p.m. and the night air was cool. The aroma of the roast lamb I had in the oven wafted down the stairs. All of a sudden Sam's face appeared between the tea towels I was hanging out.

'Ah, Mum, I've … ah … finished editing your book, and ah … well, there are a lot of spelling mistakes. I've marked in red where you need to make changes', he said with a note of authoritative pleasure in his voice.

He had taken me completely by surprise. I had thought he had lost interest and that I was going to have to find someone else to edit it for me.

'Thanks, sweetheart, I know my spelling and grammar are not the best', I smiled at him in gratitude, my heart pounding.

'No, it's not very good, Mum, I had to make a lot of changes', he smiled with delight knowing that he was now just being a smarty pants.

He hung around with me for a while talking to our dog asking her how her day had been. It became obvious to me he had something else to say, so I knew just to stay quiet and let him say what he wanted to in his own time.

'Oh yeah, Mum, and ah … there's something else – about this book. Well, um …' He paused and gave the dog a final pat and turned to look at me.

'Sam, I am really keen for your feedback. I won't be upset. You can be honest with me. I do want to know', I reassured him as I put the peg back in the basket, feeling that what he wanted to say was not easy for him. I felt afraid.

'Well, Mum, I … ah … well', he paused and then swallowed hard, 'I really like you.'

◎ Workout **17**

Being vulnerable

Safe people in my life are essential for my emotional well-being. If I do not have any safe people in my life yet, I will seek out a professional person to listen to me during my vulnerable and insecure times.

◎ ◎ ◎ ◎ ◎

It is human to feel vulnerable at different times in my life. Everybody experiences this fragile state when change takes place. Unexpected, expected and even sought-after changes will stretch me emotionally.

◎ ◎ ◎ ◎ ◎

If I have a safe person to help me during times of change I will eventually establish my emotional centre of gravity and be confident in assisting another through a similar process.

◎ ◎ ◎ ◎ ◎

Just as a person who is physically vulnerable after an injury or who is mastering a new skill sometimes needs extra support, I too need support during times of emotional vulnerability. It is wise to ask for emotional support. Remembering this will help me continue to build my levels of emotional fitness and continue to grow and learn.

◎ ◎ ◎ ◎ ◎

I will also remember that safe dolphin people will see the courage it took to share my truth, and will honour me. If I am being dishonoured or shamed for speaking my truth, having first checked my extra mile points (see Chapter 4), I will remove myself from the other person's presence and use the experience as a valuable lesson, remembering that that person may not be comfortable with their own truth and that

handling someone else's truth may have put them in
emotional overload. When people attack it is because they are
in pain.

◎ ◎ ◎ ◎ ◎

**I will remember that allowing myself to be vulnerable with
safe people helps me to:**

- hear my own heart
- accept myself
- release pain so that I don't have to carry it around
- build honest and open relationships.

18. Responsible anger

It's my rule never to lose me temper
Till it would be detrimental to keep it.

Sean O'Casey

I had self-published my first book. It was photocopied and spirally bound, with a different coloured ribbon for each character tied to the spine as a bookmark. I was very proud of our homemade handiwork. My dear friend, Prue, and I had sat for hours tying each ribbon on by hand.

I had a meeting with a major bookstore chain in Brisbane to talk about stocking my book in their stores. It had already had some television coverage and this had aroused their interest.

I took a deep breath as I pulled into their car park. I closed my eyes and thought of the little girl inside me. I focused on her being good enough and deserving of this opportunity.

The half-hour scheduled meeting lasted almost two hours and I felt as though I had made new friends as I left their office. They were keen to carry my book in all of their ten stores. I was numb.

As I drove away, tears started to run down my cheeks. My eyes were filling so fast with tears that I could not blink them away as I drove. I had to pull over. I turned into a side street and parked the car. I put my head on the steering wheel and began to sob. I was so confused.

All my life, I had been told by my father that I was dumb, that I would not be an academic and would have to marry the first man who asked me. I believed him, for as a child my dyslexia had not been diagnosed so I did not learn well and failed most subjects. I was always in awe of others who achieved academically. I left school at age fourteen and did not finish Grade 10, so I did not even receive a junior certificate. But I could type well – my fingers just knew what to do. So I went to secretarial college, but dropped out of that as well.

How could someone of my low intellect have a book on shelves in bookstores around the state? My father could not have been wrong. How can dumb people achieve? I was angry and so upset. I rang Barbara but could hardly speak. I told her about the bookstores' decision to put my book on their shelves. She congratulated me, but that seemed to only make me angrier. To contemplate that I was perhaps not dumb meant that my father must have been wrong. And if he was wrong about that, what else had he been wrong about? Maybe I was smart, maybe I was not weak, and maybe I could make something of myself?

The book was in the stores for two weeks when it made the top ten bestsellers list. I cut the list out of the newspaper and still have the cutting today. It was at number eight. I did not care that it was not the number one bestseller. To be on the list was a fantastic achievement for me, especially because my little book was homemade. The following week it climbed to number four. It was during that week that I received a concerned phone call from the manager of one of the inner-city stores.

'Cynthia, I had a disturbing phone call about you from a woman, which was left on our answering machine last night. She sounds unwell, but I think you had better come in and listen to it anyway. She says she knows you.' The manager assured me that the call would have no impact on my arrangement with them. They just thought I would like to know about it.

My heart was pumping. Who was this woman and what had she said? I was on my way to give a presentation later that morning so I left home early so that I could hear the tape first.

I arrived at their head office and was greeted by the manager. 'Cynthia, she sounds drunk or stoned. It's quite a cowardly message – she left it around 10 p.m. last night so she didn't even have the courage to speak to anyone. I wouldn't worry about it, but I just wanted you to be aware of it. She obviously has issues with you', she said as she placed the tape in the answering machine and pressed play.

'I used to be a neighbour of Cynthia Morton.' She spat my name out as if it were an obscenity. 'And let me tell you this woman is a fraud. She is neither a drug addict nor an alcoholic and has ripped her ex-husband off financially. I sometimes purchase books from your stores and you seem to be an ethical organisation. I just thought you should know who this woman really is', she slurred.

I knew who it was straight away. It was as though someone had just poured concrete inside my body. I went cold. My heart pounded. I was very surprised and deeply hurt. It was Judy.

Judy had an easily recognisable voice. It was very deep from years of heavy drug smoking. Her father was an alcoholic and she was an ex-heroin addict. She used to often speak of her father's rotten teeth when she used to visit him as a child.

Like many children of alcoholics they become drug users because they believe it makes them different from their parents. I often say to people I am working with in drug and alcohol rehabilitation groups that addiction is addiction, as there can be snobbery and elitism between the drug-taker and the alcoholic. I believe we are no different from a group of people at a weight loss clinic; it makes no difference if it was fried chicken or ice cream that they consumed to excess. Focusing on the substance is just a form of denial. In fact a statistic released by the Queensland Intravenous Aids Association showed that 92 percent of all intravenous drug addicts had alcoholic parents. They just don't want to be like their parents, but have physical dependence issues just the same.

Judy did not want to be like her father, so she did not drink much, but took drugs every day. She had been clean from heroin for years and tried to convince me when I was in my first few weeks of recovery that I did not have an alcohol problem. She knew alcoholics first-hand and I was not one of them. I did not have rotten teeth for a start. And I was definitely not a drug addict because I had never used heroin with her and as far as she was concerned anything other than heroin did not qualify as a drug.

I did much of my drinking and drugs behind closed doors. The speed I used was prescription drugs; marijuana was the same as tobacco for me – I used to steal from Joe's stash while he was at work. To the outside world I was a party girl, and of course all of our friends partied hard. Judy included.

The anger in me began to rise. I was furious. I wanted to knock on her door and punch her out. The stuff about my ripping off my ex-husband also infuriated me. I had left him with everything. He lived in our house. I rented as a single mother on a pension without a cent from him. I sold my wedding rings to pay my rent. Joe has since apologised to me for 'playing the victim', but he had obviously not told our friends that during that time of hurting he went through he had lied about the reality of our situation. How dare she? God, I was angry!

I thanked them for informing me and went on my way. It seemed ironic to me that when you told the world the truth about your flaws, some people wanted to deny them. It was confronting to them – if I were an addict, then what did that make those people who used more than I did?

I was crying and grateful for the long drive ahead of me to the presentation, so I would have some time to calm down. I grabbed the steering wheel with both hands, squeezing it as tightly as I could.

'Aaaaaarghhhh!' I was so upset. The worst part for me was that I had loved Judy, and her husband and kids. We had lived in the same neighbourhood for almost ten years. We celebrated birthdays together, and Christmas; we went on family holidays and often had dinner parties. I was so sad that she felt so much malice towards me.

I rang Brad. 'I think I should just go around there and ask her what she thinks she is doing. I have worked so hard to get to this point. Why is she trying to wreck my chances, what's in it for her to hurt me?' I asked him, searching for an answer that made sense.

'The last thing you do is go around there, Cynthia. You will just lose it, you are too angry. This woman needs to be dealt with as she is trying to defame you and that is illegal. We take the appropriate action by sending her a legal letter warning her that we will take further action if she continues. We could sue her for damages if this has affected your capacity to sell your books in any way. I will ring Lindsay, our solicitor, and get things underway. You have every right to be angry, but let's remain balanced and handle this professionally. What do you think?' The sound of his voice had calmed me. I knew he was right.

'Yes, I would probably just knock on her door and cry and ask her why, because Brad I really love her – we had so many good times together. I just don't understand why she has turned so nasty.' I was bewildered, but deep down I understood that she saw me as a traitor to our lifestyle, and wanted me to pay.

I gave a powerful speech later that morning and, if anything, used the anger to motivate rather than immobilise me.

We sent her the letter, and never heard from her again. But I bumped into her husband at my mailbox about a year later. He was a gentle man who I also cared about deeply. I was walking towards him and we made eye contact before we registered who each other was.

'Hi, Don, how are you?' I smiled as we passed each other. I could see sadness in his eyes. He smiled back, and then looked at the ground and kept walking.

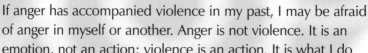 Workout **18**

Responsible anger

Anger is often easier to feel than sadness, fear or grief. The adrenalin my body releases with anger can make me feel empowered, and that is preferable to feeling the vulnerability that accompanies sadness, fear or grief. Usually underneath anger lies one of these emotions.

If anger has accompanied violence in my past, I may be afraid of anger in myself or another. Anger is not violence. It is an emotion, not an action; violence is an action. It is what I do with my anger that will either increase or decrease my level of emotional fitness.

If I lash out verbally or physically at myself or another I will cause emotional damage. This is what aggressive people do. They attempt to intimidate others or punish themselves. I do not respect people who attempt to intimidate me and I will depress myself if I punish another or deprive myself from feeling a healthy human emotion. Some people act out with their anger; others take it out on themselves. I will be aware of how I handle my anger today.

Anger is a primal response to help me protect myself or another from possible physical or emotional danger. Anger is not wrong or bad but an indicator that I need to assert my boundaries and let the other party know that their behaviour is not okay with me. I will be most effective if I am assertive, not aggressive. My dolphin is about assertion, my shark is about aggression. I have a choice how I wish to respond to anger today.

Possible verbal dialogue I can use to assert myself if I become angry today:
I don't deserve this ... I will not communicate with you until you are rational ... You need to leave me alone ... If you do that again, I will take legal action ... Please explain why you need to do this?

19. Hope or expectation?

Life's under no obligation to give us what we expect.

Margaret Mitchell

It was a big week when my little self-published book climbed to number four on the top ten bestseller list. Even though Judy's phone call had put a bit of a dampener on my excitement, once I had sent the legal letter to her I then allowed myself to digest this wonderful new reality. People were buying my book; it had worth.

I wondered what would happen to it during the fourth week – would it continue to go up or go down? I had such great hopes for my book's future. Then the phone call came.

'Cynthia, we are closing our stores; the company has gone into liquidation. Administrators will be handling the financial matters and we have many creditors. I cannot guarantee you will be paid for your sales', the manager's secretary explained.

'So you mean all the books I have sold I may never be reimbursed for?' I replied with a huge lump in my throat, holding back tears.

'That's right. It's too early to tell. Have you got a pen? I will give you the number for our administrators so that you can get more information.' She now sounded as though she was on automatic pilot; I wondered how many of these phone calls she had made this morning.

I hung up the phone and cried. The shark inside my head did the old 'I told you so routine – nothing good will ever happen for you, nothing good will ever last, it will always be taken away from you because you don't really deserve it.'

I felt so angry with myself for allowing myself to have hope that maybe I could make something of my life, that maybe if I tried hard and took responsibility for all my mistakes that somehow I would be able to attract good things into my life like other women do, and keep them. I so wanted to achieve for myself, to make a difference in the world, even if it was just with a little book.

My main concern was that I had a $5000 debt for the books. Barbara had lent me this money to pay for the book's production. I felt sure that the sales of the book would mean that I could pay her back and maybe even make enough money to print some more. My heart sank. The fear of owing money made me feel powerless, and guilty – guilty for having roped her into my dream.

'Barb, the bookstore has gone into liquidation. I don't know how I am going to pay you back. I will, but I just don't know how long it will take me. I am so sorry, Barb, I really thought it was going to work.' I cried as I explained the new turn of events to her over the phone.

'Love, that's all right, things will work out. You haven't been brought this far to be dropped now. Mother Nature knows what she is doing. When one door shuts, another one opens, love. This is just some faith homework for you. I have complete faith in you and your writing. Something better is around the corner, you just wait and see.' Her voice was as gentle and soothing as a warm bath. The sound of her words made me smile through my tears. I was astounded at her faith in my ability to do well. I wondered if she was a little naïve.

The next morning I was in the shower when I got an internal nudge to get on the phone and call some publishing houses and tell them about my book. The instructions were so clear, just like the time I knew to enter the Amazon competition. I understood intuitively that I must act – today. I cut my shower short and got out and dried myself. My heart was pumping.

I had never expected the bookstore chain to go broke, and I had never dared to hope that my book could do well outside my hometown of Brisbane. But things had changed. Maybe a national publishing house might be interested? My hope had returned.

I understood that not having an agent and my son, Sam, being the editor was working against me. I knew that my book was not a polished product by any stretch of the imagination, but it must have had some value otherwise people would not have purchased it. My dolphin was talking loudly to me. I kept speaking to myself as Barb would if she had been in the room. One door shuts so another can open; stop standing and yelling at the shut door and look around you for a better way.

What I knew of the publishing world was that big national and inter-national houses did not usually accept unsolicited manuscripts – that meant someone without an agent just sending them their work. I knew that even if I could get someone to agree to have a look at my book, it would probably sit in a six-month queue on someone's desk. It was a long shot but worth a try.

It was on about the fourth phone call I made that a receptionist actually consented to put me through to an editor's secretary. All of the previous calls were terminated as soon as they knew I did not have an agent.

'One moment, I am transferring you now, hold please', she said in a swanky Sydney voice. Sydney is a hip, slick and cool place compared to Brisbane; it is a little like the New York of Australia. They speak faster and smile less, and the women, especially, seem ballsier to me. My heart was pounding. God, what was I going to say?

'Yes, can I help you?' the woman asked in a clipped English accent.

'My name is Cynthia Morton. I self-published a book up here in Brisbane and it was put into a bookstore chain and got onto the top ten bestseller list – well it climbed from number eight to number four within a couple of weeks. That bookstore chain has now gone into liquidation … And well, my book must have some appeal because it sold really well.' I paused for a minute for her to interject, but there was just silence so I kept speaking.

'I am a recovering drug addict and alcoholic and survivor of childhood abuse. I wrote this book to help myself make sense of my life so that I could get out of a loony bin, and well … not lose custody of my two boys. I would just like to send it to you because I can't afford to get any more printed … and well, what do you think?' Her silence was killing me; I wanted some feedback so I stopped speaking to give her a chance.

'For a start, I am not the editor's secretary, I am the editor. I never usually answer my secretary's phone but I was just walking past and for some strange reason I picked it up. She is not at her desk; she must be in the ladies room or somewhere. I have just returned from New York and have only just got into the office', she explained.

I was now the silent one. Had I known I was speaking to the editor I would have been way too intimidated to ramble like I had. I thought it best to just shut up and let her continue.

'Now, Cynthia is it? I think you had better pop your book in an overnight bag and address it directly to me. I need to have a look at it; it sounds very interesting. Can you do that for me?' She paused, waiting for my response.

'Sure, sure, I will do that straight away. God, thank you for taking the time to talk to me. I will get it to you straight away.' I stumbled over my words, thanking her probably too many times.

My heart was pounding. I looked up at the notice board above my computer. It is filled with many affirmations that motivate me, as well as photos of little Cynthia and other females I admire – Shirley MacLaine and Ruth Cracknell and of course my beautiful Barb. The affirmation, 'A professional writer is an amateur that didn't quit', seemed to jump out at me. I had been writing for over a decade, and finally a real editor would be looking at my work. I smiled gently at little Cynthia's four-year-old face, which was looking lovingly down at me. We were a good team – her and me.

I closed my eyes as I kissed the overnight bag before I placed it in the post box. It was out of my hands now.

A week passed and my hopes began to fade. I was walking around a shopping mall when my mobile phone rang.

'Cynthia, I won't publish anyone I don't like. I would like to fly you to Sydney to meet with me. Can you make it down next week?' It took a few minutes to register that it was the editor from the publishing house I had spoken to earlier.

'Yes, yes, I will just get my diary out. What day, when would you like me to come?' I stuttered as I frantically unloaded the contents of my handbag onto the lid of a rubbish bin outside a department store, trying to flip my diary open and hold the phone between my cheek and shoulder.

'Could you just hang on a minute. I will have to put the phone down. I won't be a sec.' I was flustered and began to drop things.

'Not a problem', she replied patiently.

I put the phone down and took a deep breath and blew it out slowly to release the anxiety I was feeling. I was standing in the middle of a crowded shopping centre having a life altering moment. People were shuffling past me oblivious to the monumental conversation I was having.

It was arranged for me to fly down the following week. I found it hard to believe that she even wanted to meet me. Working out what to wear proved to be difficult. What would a potential author wear? I had no idea. So I decided to play it safe and wear some pink. I always felt comforted and confident in pink.

As the plane rose into the air leaving Brisbane the shark in my head attempted to convince me that the plane would crash – this was definitely a too good to be true event for someone like me. It was a battle the whole way to keep believing that I had a chance to have my book published nationally, and that I was worthy of this.

As the taxi pulled up outside the huge Sydney high-rise my heart began to pound. I walked into the foyer not believing what I was seeing.

A year before, around the time of my birthday, I had a vision as I was standing in the shower. I had been released from the loony bin and my writings had started to look like a book. I was daydreaming about what it would be like to write a book, a real book that people could buy in bookshops. I was wondering about the daunting world of publishing houses that dealt with professional authors who were talented and famous. As the hot water rinsed away the shampoo suds from my hair, I closed my eyes and saw myself riding a lift in a huge building. I knew the building was not in Brisbane, perhaps Melbourne or Sydney. I was imagining I was going up to chat with my publisher about my next book. I could see the artwork in the foyer and the huge glass doors, and I could hear the city traffic. I felt like I was there. I stood frozen for a while not wanting to open my eyes for I knew the vision would disappear. Oh, what would it be like to be a success, to achieve something meaningful just because of who you are, I wondered. I got out of the shower and went on my way, brushing aside the vision as a too good to be true event for someone like me.

As I stood in the foyer of the publishing house I realised that the artwork in the foyer was exactly as I had imagined in my daydream a year before. I felt an odd rush of déjà vu and a knowing that I had seen this day's events a year before, as I had also done with the Amazon trip and the birth of my sons. I had trouble believing them and difficulty explaining them, but these visions did offer me comfort – they were almost like landmarks telling me I was on the right track.

I met with the editor and the marketing manager. We spoke for a couple of hours and at the end of our conversation the editor had tears in her eyes. I was unsure what had moved her, but it felt like a good thing. I was so pleased with myself for not having said the 'F' word at all. Sometimes when I get passionate I use it as a powerful adjective, but it's not always understood by others. In telling my truth I am not always appropriate. I had not edited myself with these women, but the need to use this colourful word had not arisen. I was grateful.

The editor then took me to lunch. We were sitting overlooking Sydney's beautiful harbour. I could see the Opera House and the bridge in all their splendour. It was a beautiful day.

'Well, Cynthia, we would like to publish your book. It would probably be about a nine-month production time, and we would be looking at a national publicity tour. We would also like to offer you royalties up front. How does $5000 sound?' she asked with delight in her eyes.

I was numb. Five thousand dollars was the exact amount I needed to pay Barbara back. I never expected this to happen – or even dared to hope.

Barbara had been right. Had the Brisbane bookstore chain not gone bankrupt I would never have sought out a national publishing house and be sitting here today with this woman offering me a publishing contract.

One door did shut for a better one to open.

◎ Workout 19

Hope or expectation?

I will remember not to confuse hope with expectation today.

◎ ◎ ◎ ◎ ◎

An expectation is about having a desire met within a certain time frame with a definite outcome. Expectations are about my desire to control and dictate to the universe how things should be, and when they should happen. It is not until I let go of control that I can truly have hope.

◎ ◎ ◎ ◎ ◎

Hope is about a heartfelt desire – it's like a dove we set free into the blue summer sky. It is safe to have hope. I deserve to have my desires met, but will understand that sometimes it is not good for me to get everything I wish for, and that I have to give time, time.

◎ ◎ ◎ ◎ ◎

If I look back at old lovers I wished for, and events that I begged the universe to make come true, I realise the blessing for me was that they did not come true. I was better off without them.

◎ ◎ ◎ ◎ ◎

I will also remember that when things go wrong it does not necessarily mean I am being punished or deprived. There is a bigger picture and not everything is about me. For example, if it rains on my wedding day, it does not mean that Mother Nature is out to get me. It just means the earth needed some rain.

◎ ◎ ◎ ◎ ◎

I will let go of expectation and feel free to hope today by remembering:
Sometimes not having dreams realised is the healthiest outcome for me … if a door shuts on me today I will not stand there and complain but look around for another opening.

20. Safe friendships

No person is your friend who demands your silence, or
denies your right to grow.

Alice Walker

'I read about you in *The Courier Mail*. We see the same shrink and, well, I'd really like to meet with you, to talk with you and do some one-on-one work with you', a soft voice said on the other end of the phone.

I had recently been featured in our local paper. It was odd seeing a picture of myself above a story about me, as if I were someone important. I liked it, but I also felt guilty. I knew where this guilt came from. I had pretended all my life that I was an idiot, that I didn't know much, that all the men in my life were smarter than I was. My undiagnosed dyslexia compounded this belief about myself. It felt wrong to feel good about myself or to dare to believe that I had something of value to say to the world. When I first saw the article, the delight I felt was quickly followed by fear. Fear of getting into trouble – telling family secrets. It was not allowed.

Last time I was interviewed in the media Joe's mother, Dulcie, had written into the television station that dared to call me an 'Australian Hero' for telling my story. Joe's mother told them that I was a liar, that I had made up the story about my childhood just to get published. She had never heard me mention it while married to Joe. She said that she was my ex-mother-in-law and knew there was no way I could be an alcoholic or drug addict.

I had never mentioned my abuse to anyone, until I got clean and sober.

Dulcie's call upset me as Judy's phone call to the bookstores had, but not as much. I knew what to do – send her the same legal letter. Dulcie and Judy had always got along well at our family get-togethers. Joe's mother also had a chronic alcohol problem. I knew nurses who had looked after her in hospital, and they had spoken to me about their concern that she always brought in a bottle of whisky to wash down the pain-killers. She had attempted suicide a few times during Joe's and my marriage. She was a wounded angry woman who was also highly intelligent. She was in Mensa – and she made it known to me that I was no intellectual giant.

The fact that I was achieving after having left Joe was obviously too much for her to bear.

I was waiting for the next attack. The first exposure with the bookstore chain had brought Judy's attack, and the first television feature had produced Dulcie's slander. I wondered who this newspaper article would bring out of the woodwork.

Barbara comforted me when I questioned her as to whether it was better to just say nothing, and not try. 'Whenever you stick your head out to achieve there will always be knockers. It's the tall poppy syndrome and it's alive and well in Australia. If you look at the people who have the hardest time with your recovery, they are all in active addiction but still living in denial. They are the ones who want to shut you up so that they don't have to look at themselves. I am proud of you, love. It takes a lot of courage to speak your truth. You may not have the support of biological family but you have a heart family now. The Mortons and Trevor and I love you and admire your strength. Don't let other people's fear silence you any more.' I held onto her words as to a life raft. I recorded them in my heart and played them back to myself over and over.

The voice on the other end of the phone speaking about the latest newspaper article I did not know. I had jumped when the phone had rung, wondering if I was about to receive a verbal attack from someone for again speaking out in the media. I did not expect encouragement or validation.

'I really admire your courage. I could never speak out like you are. I am currently in a loony bin, but could get out to meet you for a coffee. Would you have any time? My name is Sarah', she said in a familiar tone. I heard sadness in her voice. I knew that sadness, I had felt it myself.

I agreed to meet her, feeling like I was about to meet an old friend. As I pulled up outside the crowded coffee shop I saw her immediately. She was sitting alone like a little butterfly perched on a chair. The slightest movement could have startled her to fly away and never be seen again.

'Hi Sarah, I'm Cynthia, nice to meet you', I said holding out my hand to shake hers.

'Oh, God, thanks for meeting me, I feel like an idiot. I don't even really know what to say to you. I saw you in the paper and just knew I had to meet you.' She was fragile but strong. I liked her and understood her immediately.

The following week I met her in the same psychiatric hospital that I had been in just a few short years before. She had been anorexic for ten years and had almost died from her eating disorder.

'Hi Sarah', I said, entering her darkened hospital room. She could not speak. She was sitting on the floor holding onto her knees. Her hair was shorter than it had been the week before. It looked like she had butchered it with scissors. The scars on her wrists and chest were self-inflicted wounds from years of burning and cutting herself.

I sat on the floor with her and spoke about when I was in that hospital. She eventually looked at me and began to tell me her story.

She had been abused as a child by a woman – raped with instruments, cut and tortured. I had never heard such horrific detail about female abusers. Sarah felt great disgust towards herself because she was a female, hence the starvation and self-mutilation.

Months passed and we continued to share our stories. We would meet in New Farm Park, sit on the ground on a picnic blanket and look at the water. She was still abusing alcohol for the first few months that we met, but eventually stopped drinking as it began to interfere with her desire to heal.

I shared with her techniques that had helped me in my recovery. We threw wet clay at walls; she painted, cried, screamed and rocked herself in corners. She had so much pain that just needed to be let out. She needed to be heard, but most of all to hear herself so that she could get to know who she was. It was an honour to be in her presence, and to be trusted by her.

It was in the second year of working with Sarah that I realised I would love to have a female like her as a friend. She was extremely intelligent and had a photographic memory. She could speak just as fluently backwards as she could forwards. She was so gutsy and witty that I really grew to love her. And that frightened me.

I had been searching all my life for a best friend – someone I could trust, confide in, cry and laugh with. I had never found one. Women always seemed unsafe to me. I didn't trust or understand them.

I was beginning to understand from working with Sarah that until Sarah had made peace with little Sarah she would not be good company for herself. I took along photographs of little Cynthia and spoke to her about how my healing had had to start with that little girl inside me who I was terrified to acknowledge because she was in so much pain.

Little Cynthia and I had now become close. She featured on the cover of my first book. She was now my best friend – no, way more than that, I loved her, I parented, protected and supported her. I had become to her the parent she always wished she could have had. I still didn't understand many females, but I understood myself. I felt safe within my own skin for the first time in my life, and I knew that this was the journey Sarah also had to make.

Little Sarah was like a fairy. I was eventually allowed to see photographs of her and hear about her pain. She loved to do cartwheels whenever a stretch of grass was before her. Sarah is a tall woman who used to play tennis with Pat Rafter as a teenager – she is naturally athletic. To watch her long body take the shape of a star as she did one cartwheel after another was a beautiful sight to see, especially as it was followed with a genuine smile of self-satisfaction when she had finished. The more I got to know about the whole person that was Sarah, the more fun we had and the closer we became.

We often spoke about running a free community centre for people like us. We would have an art room and a clay throwing room, a massage component, support groups to which people could come and be understood. There would be no talk of religion and no judgement; it would be a safe place.

As the years passed, Sarah and I were successful in gaining a government grant and we piloted a program we called 'Emotional Fitness'. We offered art classes, massage, acting, yoga and support groups. We were asked if we thought we could attract ten people to work with us so that they could film a documentary about the processes we used. We had 90 people through our doors in three months and 29 agencies using our services. The documentary that was filmed won first prize at a national Australian film festival.

Sarah and I have become beautiful friends, although somehow the word 'friend' does not adequately describe the bond we share. We are both born in the Chinese horoscope's Year of the Tiger – exactly twelve years apart. We are strong women who complement each other; there is no competition, but a genuine desire to help each other find our souls' wings and fly. I did not know that women could have relationships like this. We both still see the same shrink and are still works in progress, so I look forward to our fifties and sixties together when all the healing is complete.

I never thought I would feel safe enough to walk arm-in-arm with another woman, or hug her and tell her I loved her without a few bottles of champagne under my belt.

I am truly happy for her as she succeeds. Her beautiful chocolate brown hair has now grown past her shoulders. She stands strong and tall as she addresses female students on being true to themselves – at a school from which she had once been expelled.

It was not until I became a good friend to myself that I could be a good friend to anyone else and attract beautiful women like Sarah into my heart and my life.

◎ Workout **20**

Safe friendships

I will remember today that unless I am a caring friend to myself it is impossible for me to maintain a long-term quality friendship with another.

◎ ◎ ◎ ◎ ◎

Until I am loyal to myself, patient and flexible, I will be unable to give those gifts to another.

◎ ◎ ◎ ◎ ◎

A true friend would not ask me to betray myself for them. I will not ask others to betray themselves for me.

◎ ◎ ◎ ◎ ◎

I feel safe with others who can see the humorous side of themselves and life, who care and who are unafraid to show their feelings. Am I that person for my friends?

◎ ◎ ◎ ◎ ◎

If I need to cry today the safest person to cry with would be someone who would not try to silence me or fix me. Someone who would listen and encourage me to speak my truth is the safest company for me. I choose to be that person for another if they need me today.

◎ ◎ ◎ ◎ ◎

Safe friendships mean:

- not having to perform or pretend for another's approval
- not having to be silent or edit the truth for fear of their rejection
- not having to be happy and 'together' all the time.

21. Dealing with the ex-partner

*Do you suppose if a wound goes real deep the healing of it
can hurt almost as bad as what caused it?*

Lee David Zlotoff

Every second weekend the boys would come home and bring their father's energy in the door with them. Transition time! I hated it.

After two days with him they would take on some of his personality traits, sayings and habits such as dissecting movies they had seen with him and the holes in the plot. I knew from having lived with Joe for years when the boys were subconsciously parroting his words.

It tore at my heart. They got the best of him and I got the worst. It was an insult to them to put him down, but it insulted me when they pumped him up.

I remembered all too well how I had lost respect for my mother every time she character-assassinated my father. My father did nothing for us after he left. He did not help her out financially in any way. She hated him, but we kids still loved him. Kids love both, no matter what – they are dolphins – unless of course one parent threatens to emotionally leave them unless they take sides. Then a child's survival mechanism will kick in because they instinctively know they need love and they will do what is necessary to keep at least one person loving them.

'Do you want us to hate him, Mum? To think he's an arsehole like you do? Is that what you want? Because I don't!' I cringed as those words came out of Mitchell's mouth.

Yes, I wanted them to see his faults; yes, I wanted them to realise how tired I got from never having time off during school holidays, how Joe's work could never be interrupted but mine could; yes, I was angry with him for relinquishing responsibility, for leaving all the parenting up to Brad and me.

This was a man who used to hit me, who chose a loyalty to drugs over our marriage, who was condescending and sexist, who I used to adore. These days I can't stand the sight of him. I don't like him at all.

How did I get to be such an angry woman when it comes to him? Why do I get so mad?

Because I expected more, I didn't hope, I expected, forgetting that wise saying that 'Life is under no obligation to give us what we expect.' And whenever I get mad these days it is because I have entertained expectations once more – therein lies the reason for my cycle of anger and disappointment.

The boys had told me Joe was going on holidays. I was so jealous. I needed a holiday. We could not afford a holiday. We had just sent Sam to Germany and would not be having a break this year.

I saw so many other divorced couples at least share the parenting time over school holidays, but not us. Joe was too busy. And when he had a partner in his life, he had less time.

The guilt I felt for wanting a break from the boys from time to time was immense. They had always been easy kids, but their energy in the house when I was trying to write was so invasive. The washing, the cooking, the shopping, the noise, the money for movies, it never seemed to end.

I have felt so dysfunctional over the years when it comes to my ex. I remember a shrink once telling me never to put down the boys' dad to them. They see themselves as a part of him, so if I put him down, I am putting them down. Young boys want to be like their father, approved of and admired by their father, and they want their mother to love their father, and love them.

It is so hard when you don't like the person your children's other parent has become – to not be false or dishonour yourself by pretending, but in being honest, not to hurt them either.

I still find this one of my most challenging emotional workouts.

'I know it's your stuff, Mum. I don't take it on', Sam said to me in the midst of my losing it because poor Joe needed a holiday. One part of me was pleased that Sam could remove himself from my pain and realise he was not responsible; the other part of me, my shark, wanted him to be angry with his father for hurting me and letting me down over the years like he had.

Oh what I victim I could be. And I loved it, wanting my children to takes sides, to gang up with me to make me feel better. Oh, my mother, myself!

When I occasionally fall off my emotional bike because I lose my centre of gravity from too many expectations I sometimes need help to get back on it again. All I know is that writing about it helps. Talking to Barbara and to my shrink about it also helps.

It is neither of my sons' responsibility to take care of my wounding and insecurities. I am the adult.

I need to remember that if Joe and I were good at understanding each other and working things out we probably wouldn't have separated.

'I just want you to shut up about him, Mum, I don't want to hear it', Mitchell said one day with tears in his eyes.

Thank God that he could be honest with me. At times when I was dysfunctional and unloading my pain onto him, he asserted himself and protected himself from my pain. I would never have dared to do that with my mother. I felt responsible for her pain; I made her pain mine.

My boys knew the difference and they had personal boundaries they were not afraid to assert. They seemed to use the emotional fitness techniques around me when I had forgotten them.

I know it's a blessing that Joe chose a life using drugs over a life with me and the boys because, if he had not, I would never have met myself and all the beautiful dolphins I have in my life today.

I just forget to count my blessings sometimes.

◎ Workout **21**

Dealing with your ex-partner

I will remember that acceptance is the key to peace of mind
when it comes to my ex. Acceptance does not mean submission. I don't have to like my ex's behaviour, but I do have to
accept that we don't get along and find peace in that reality.

◎ ◎ ◎ ◎ ◎

Just because two people do not get along it does not automatically mean that one party is wrong and the other is right.
They may just be different.

◎ ◎ ◎ ◎ ◎

It is important for me not to become self-righteous and
superior. Just because my emotional taste buds don't enjoy my
ex-partner any more, it does not mean that anyone else who
does enjoy them is immediately wrong.

◎ ◎ ◎ ◎ ◎

When it comes to the children I am best to take out my anger
and frustration with another adult, not with them. It is not
their responsibility to look after my needs. It is dysfunctional
and unfair of me to expect them to take sides. I will ultimately
lose the respect of my children if I emotionally bully them into
agreeing with me.

◎ ◎ ◎ ◎ ◎

What my ex-partner does in his or her private life is none of
my business any more. I am out of balance when I am asking
my children questions about their time with my ex just so I
can get information. I need to check my motive when I ask
them how they enjoyed their time away.

◎ ◎ ◎ ◎ ◎

It will help me to remember that every human being has assets and liabilities.

I will remember the following when it comes to my ex-partner:

I am no longer their partner ... What they do is none of my business unless it endangers my child ... I will remember not to be surprised that we cannot communicate well as that is one of the main reasons we are no longer together.

22. Beautiful sexual intimacy

Intimacy takes time. If I don't have time, I probably won't have intimacy.

Anne Wilson Schaef

'Cynthia, there will come a day when you will find having sex a beautiful experience, you will feel good afterwards, not dirty – and you will even be able to laugh, smile and look into the eyes of the one who is making love to you', my shrink said, attempting to comfort me.

'Yeah, right!' I scoffed. I felt sick and embarrassed by his words. It seemed like a mission impossible for me since I had become clean and sober. I had never been sexually intimate with a male without the aid of booze or drugs. It was proving such a huge and overwhelming ordeal in recovery that I just wanted to give up trying. It all seemed like a bad joke. Surely it wasn't supposed to be this hard – no wonder people drink and take drugs.

Brad is a patient man. In the early days I was medicating on chocolate, literally almost inhaling the stuff. I would get so high on sugar I would be able to numb myself emotionally. Chocolate became my new drug. It wasn't nearly as effective as drugs and alcohol, but it helped a little – physical distractions such as feeling sick on chocolate were great emotional avoidance strategies, but only short-term.

Many a time Brad would start to rub my tummy, looking at me with desire in his eyes, and I would clam up.

The poor man was consistently getting knocked back or we would be deep in foreplay and I would have a horrifying flashback and curl up into a ball and cry. He would just stroke my hair and comfort me.

'I just love holding you, it doesn't matter. This stuff will work itself out in time', he would say, pulling the blankets up over my shoulders and kissing my cheek.

'You're only with me for sex, that's all you really want from me, isn't it?' I would say accusingly.

'Sweetheart, no offence, but if I was interested in a woman just for sex I would not have chosen you. You're pretty wounded in that area. I am with you for you.'

I could not work that one out. With me for me? I was a shipwreck of a human being – there was no me. Who was this 'me' he was talking about? I wanted to meet her. I felt like the hole in a donut; without drugs and alcohol I felt like I did not exist.

He had been a bachelor by choice for many years. Previous girl-friends had given him books on commitment because he liked being footloose. Why had he committed to me? I could not work it out; maybe he had just become desperate.

But he was persistent. He was a great endurance swimmer, he competed in triathlons and he liked challenges – he certainly had one in me!

In hindsight, I eventually began to see a pattern emerge. I had been stalked and preyed upon sexually throughout my formative years, never honoured. I never got to say no and be listened to. My soul was hungry for that opportunity and that respect. It was the only thing that would heal me. It was as if every wound that my heart had endured from being dishonoured had to be tended to with the reverse. To be honoured was the cure, but it was extremely painful. Like disinfectant on a wound. I winced and pulled away always at first. I am so grateful that Brad did not give up on me. His love kept gently bathing my wounds.

The pattern seemed to be that I would need to say no to his sexual advances perhaps three, even four times in a row and not be shamed or abandoned. Every time he held me as I cried.

'I am so sorry. I just can't. There is something wrong with me. It will be at least twenty years before I can ever have sex again, if ever. I am not teasing you, I promise; I don't mean to hurt you. I just can't do this – I'm a mess', I would say through my tears with my back to him.

'It's okay, I've survived twenty years without you before. Come here and put your head on my chest and have a good cry', he would say with humour in his voice.

My twenty years seemed to be just a few weeks and I would allow myself to surrender to the overwhelming feeling of love I had for him. And when we had sex it did not feel like sex as it took time, sometimes hours, for me to feel sufficiently safe. It was more a spiritual experience that encompassed all of me – like someone who had been kept locked up in the dark, I could only tolerate a little sunshine at a time. But it felt like way too long to ask a man to wait – a few weeks! I grew up with the belief that women had a sexual quota they had to fulfil per week to keep a man at home. And I know that that is the case for some couples whose relationships have nothing else of interest to sustain them between interludes.

What I did not know was that there were also relationships that were about quality rather than quantity. Barbara was teaching me that. She had been with her husband for almost 30 years and she still had a twinkle in her eye when she spoke of him. Or when they were together, he would just come up behind her and throw his arms around her waist and kiss her neck, and she'd smile like a young schoolgirl. God I wanted that.

'It's about intimacy, love, and that saying that explains intimacy as 'in-to-me-see' sums it up perfectly. Not until the one you love has seen into your heart and knows its wounding and its strengths can you truly make love, feel love and be loved. Only then it becomes about the human being, not the body; about the experience, the journey, not the orgasm. Holding each other, seeing each other, respecting each other, having fun and being playful with each other – that is how one makes love', she explained with such grace and wisdom. And I knew it to be true because I had seen it in her eyes and I had watched her live it in her life.

Every time I said no and Brad honoured me, one small wound was healed. It took time, baby steps and repetition.

It was as though I had to go back and reclaim every part of myself that was wounded, tend to it, clean the wound, let the scab form and be tender for a while, let the scab fall off in its own time to let the scar tissue form, and only then the wound would heal. Emotional scar tissue is a lot easier to cope with than an open infected wound.

It took about three years together before I caught myself one morning feeling great. I was naked and so was Brad. I had him pinned down on the bed trying to hold him there for a few more minutes before he had to get up to go for his morning swim. I just wanted to play with him some more. We were laughing and giggling like children, so much so that there were tears running down my cheeks. I felt beautiful, I felt empowered, I felt sexually strong and healthy. I had met the 'me' he was talking about, and I was beginning to enjoy her company too.

My shrink had been right. What had seemed like mission impossible I could now chalk up to – mission accomplished.

I had made my scars my stars.

◎ Workout **22**

Beautiful sexual intimacy

I will remember the breakdown of the word intimacy today, in-to-me-see. If I desire beautiful sexual intimacy I must be brave enough to allow the other person to see into me. I must be brave enough to show my heart.

I will also remember that it is impossible to be intimate with another unless there is trust. And trust for some people, especially the emotionally wounded, takes time to build. I will be patient with myself and give time, time.

Sometimes eye contact helps in giving a reading as to how emotionally available the other person is. If my partner is unable to look me in the eye, and have the lights on while we are having sex, it is an indicator that maybe their heart is not engaged. It is simply a physical transaction they are looking for. If this is not what I am looking for I will be honest with myself and not entertain unhealthy expectations.

If I am afraid or overwhelmed, I will remember to be honest with myself and not force myself to have sex if my heart is not in it. I will also respect my partner if they say that they are not in the mood.

Sexual appetites are as individual as physical appetites and I will remember not to shame myself or my partner if we are not sexually hungry at the same time.

It may help me to remember what beautiful sexual intimacy is by refreshing my memory as to what it is not:
Sex is not an obligation, but a desire ... It is not degrading or demanding ... It is not an indicator as to my worth as a human being ... Intimacy takes time, I will slow down today.

23. Giving and receiving affection

Tenderness is greater proof of love than the most passionate of vows.

Marlene Dietrich

Her hands have a soft talcum powder feel to them. The skin on them is as soft as a newborn baby's tummy. When she touches me I want to cry, and sometimes I do. I am so thirsty for that maternal 'I care about you' sort of touch.

Barbara was the first person to teach me about affection. I did not really understand what it was until I met her. I knew about attention and that was about as close as I came to understanding it. Just someone listening to me or looking at me seemed to fill a void. I was desperate to be known, understood and cherished – for someone to find me really interesting, captivating, for them to seek me out because they just liked to be with me. Not because of the way I cooked dinner, or gossiped, or because I was convenient and they were lonely, but because I enriched their lives just by being myself. She showed me that I enriched her life with her generous displays of affection.

I used to think that those fleeting cheek kisses that friends socially offered me was affection, or Joe wanting to have sex with me, or a drunk girlfriend linking arms with me as we staggered along, or a best friend's husband's kiss – that was what I thought affection was between adults.

My boys of course always showed me affection. Their little moist kisses and their small hands inside of mine as we crossed the road were true gifts of affection when they were small, but I found them so uncomfortable. I was fine with giving them kisses and cuddles, but I was always the first to pull away, especially if they were the instigator. I would become overwhelmed and quickly make the housework I was in the middle of doing more important – a self-justifying excuse not to have to receive their pure hearts. Their affection brought up fear within me. I remembered what it was like to need a parent's validation of a safe touch and tender words and glances – it brought up too much pain from the past.

It was Barbara's touch that began my heart's thawing. Her divine hands and the energy that radiated from them was only one dimension of how she conveyed her affection.

When I would tell her about finishing a chapter of my book, or receiving a government grant to help fund a free community centre, or how I had resolved a parenting issue or surrendered to a fear that was holding me back with Brad, she would let a tear roll down her cheek. Her eyes often filled with tears when we spoke. She was the first person I could smile with as she became teary. I knew they were tears of joy. I had never met anyone who cried tears of joy and gratitude until I met her.

Her voice on the other end of the phone when I was upset was another display of her affection. When she knew I was in turmoil or really afraid her voice would become like a cashmere shawl that she would throw around my shoulders even if she were miles away from me on an interstate work trip.

I remembered the first time she linked arms with mine as we walked one day. I was shocked and very moved – such a fearless public display of affection. She not only linked arms but patted the back of my hand as she spoke. And she was sober! I wanted her to never let me go. Now sometimes before I go on stage to speak to a large audience we hold hands. Her affection charges my heart and reminds me that I am lovable – it has saved my life. I now show this affection to women I love.

It was only through Barb's demonstrations of affection that I came to understand what it was and could translate it into my relationship with Brad and then other adult females.

One of my beautiful friends is Prue. She is Barb's age and it is divine to be in her presence. She is a Rubenesque type of woman, ripe and round with a wonderful sense of style and colour. She wraps a fuchsia pink shawl around her tanned shoulders, throws on a pair of Jackie O sunglasses and a hat, and makes an entrance wherever she goes. Her energy is of vanilla and lavender. She smells wonderful and also has feminine, beautiful hands like Barb. Prue swims a lot and lives by the ocean; I call her a mermaid and even did an oil painting of her one year for her birthday. She, too, has comforting maternal energy.

One day we were working together in a recovery group when I had some grief arise about my mother. I was very sad and overwhelmed about some event in my past. Little Cynthia inside me needed to be held and comforted. Prue was sitting cross-legged on the floor wearing divine white Capri pants that had huge red cherries hand-painted all over them. It took so much courage to move towards her and put my head in her lap. It was like moving against gravity to get to her, but I eventually did, and rested my cheek on her soft thigh and sobbed.

'Oh, my darling, let it out, let it out, I love you, and I will always be here for you', she gently said as she tucked my hair behind my ear and stroked my forehead.

I cried in her lap, curling my legs up into a foetal ball. She rocked me. 'It's all right, my darling, you're not alone any more.'

Her gentle affection helped me move through a great deal of pain that had presented itself that day. Genuine affection – I never knew it was such a subtle but powerful healer.

For me, giving affection is easier than receiving it because if I am the giver I am in control; however, if I have to receive I then have to allow myself to surrender and feel worthy to receive. That's where all my discomfort had come from – feeling unworthy.

My shrink gave me good advice when I was first trying to increase my level of emotional fitness around giving and receiving affection. 'Whenever your boys or someone you care about hugs you, try and be the last one to pull away. That is a really effective workout. Notice how you are feeling – the discomfort is about your self-worth. Allowing affection into your life is one of the most nourishing exercises you can do to promote self-worth', he would assure me repetitively during our sessions.

Sam had been overseas on a German exchange trip with his school earlier this year. He had been home a day or so and was chatting to me in the kitchen late in the evening – the rest of the family was in bed.

'I love you, Mum', he said as he walked towards me with outstretched arms, signalling that he wanted a hug. He is a huge young man, standing 196 centimetres tall.

His need for me to hug him was overwhelming. He now seemed so independent and grown up I was beginning to feel a little redundant.

'I love you too, sweetheart', I replied as I pressed my cheek into the soft side of his neck where his pulse tickled my cheek. As we stood there in the silence of the house, I decided I would not pull away, I would let him hug me as long as he needed to, remembering Mal's words of advice.

We stood there for a long time – minutes. His huge, puppy-like body had the same beautiful energy as it did when I held him in my arms when he was a little baby almost seventeen years ago. I could feel the strength of his body; he was no longer a boy, but a man, a gentle man unafraid of being tender. I felt so small next to him, but realised that my love and affection was still important to him, and he was wise enough to know when he needed affection, and brave enough to seek it out.

Tears welled up in my eyes. I had not realised how much I needed this exchange of affection and surrendered to the vulnerable beauty that comes with expressing love.

◎ Workout **23**
Giving and receiving affection

Human touch that communicates caring is called affection. Today I will make an attempt to consciously give and receive affection.

If I am hugged today by a child or an adult, I will make a note not to pull away first. I will let the other person hold on to me for as long as they need to.

If someone I care about attempts to kiss me today, I will not divert my eyes or turn my cheek. I will look directly at them before or after they kiss me and smile. If I choose to kiss someone today I will make eye contact before or after the kiss and give them a whole-face smile.

I will ask someone I care about if I can give them a hug out of the blue. If they say no, I will not take offence but will tell them that they have one in credit if they need it later.

I will take the hand of someone I care about today and hold it for a moment in silence.

◎ ◎ ◎ ◎ ◎

I will speak to those I care about affectionately before they start their day and at the close of their day.

◎ ◎ ◎ ◎ ◎

Some affectionate words I may choose to use today:

I care about you … I enjoy your company … I am thinking of you … I am glad you are in my life … Would you like a hug?

24. Understanding emotionally unavailable people

If you want others to be happy, practise compassion
If you want to be happy, practise compassion.

Dalai Lama

It was my first time in Melbourne and I was to do a morning television show. I was excited. As I made my way out of the sliding glass doors at the airport to the taxi rank, the cold air hit me. I had forgotten how cold 15°C was. Living in sunny Queensland it was rare to feel this cold at 10 a.m.

As I looked at the people ahead of me in the taxi queue I became conscious of my pink suit. Melbourne people dressed in very dark colours it seemed. Charcoal grey, black and navy suits surrounded me. My shark attempted to taunt me with thoughts of self-doubt, but I quickly changed head tapes as my dolphin assured me that my pink suit was just divine. I agreed, I just looooove pink.

As I sat in the make-up chair at the television studio I felt like a child again. My mother would sit me on the kitchen table and put perming rollers in my hair at four years of age. I knew to sit still and just let her do what she wanted to me. I was always uncomfortable around make-up artists and hairdressers. I felt so powerless. I had not yet worked up the courage to tell them that I never wear eye shadow and, quite frankly, I think it looks ridiculous on my face.

The young girl picked up what looked like a spray gun and tested it on the back of her hand.

'Hmmm, this colour will be great on your skin tone', she told me as she began to spray my neck.

I could not believe it. It was a spray gun like you see at a panel beater's shop. As I watched my face become flawless, my heart sank. I liked my imperfections, my freckles and the smile lines around my eyes. Then she started on the eye shadow. I ended up looking like a drag queen.

'Gorgeous! You look great. Feel free to help yourself to coffee in the

Green Room; you're on in half an hour', she said as she began to pack up her equipment.

'Great, thanks. Oh, by the way, where's the ladies room?' I asked, trying not to sound too desperate.

I followed her directions, locked myself in and began to wipe away the frosty crap she had placed around my eyes. I had my own make-up bag with me and replaced the pasty pink lipstick she had painfully painted on me with my favourite gutsy pink. There was nothing I could do about the spray job. I just had to live with it.

'So, Cynthia, tell me what you're up to these days. How's life for you now?' the host asked me with what seemed like genuine interest. It was not a live show; we were filming a few days ahead of Easter Monday, so we had to pretend it was a Monday rather than a Friday.

'Well, things are good. I am married to a beautiful dolphin man now, my boys are doing well, I'm working on my next book and I've also got a great shrink!' I replied. We chatted for another few minutes then cut to a commercial break.

We were off air when he said with what seemed like astonishment, 'Cynthia, thank you so very much for mentioning in such a relaxed, matter-of-fact way that you see a shrink. It is so healthy and a part of life for many people, but so few will speak freely about it', he moved closer and looked deep into my eyes. 'You know I had a very public nervous breakdown when I was about 40. It was in all the magazines. I had become a workaholic, I was burnt out and I was not coping with my hectic life. I was put into hospital. I was a wreck.' The expression on his face changed, and I could tell that he was recalling a very difficult time in his life.

'At the same time another colleague, also in the entertainment industry, was in the same hospital, suffering from burnout like me. I am sure I was reading about him, and he about me, in all the same magazines. And then one morning I was walking down the hospital corridor and I came face to face with him. There was no escaping each other. Here were two of Australia's most recognisable faces on television in our pyjamas, broken and quite frankly feeling very lost. And you know I walked up to him pretending I did not know about his breakdown and said, "So, how are you, mate? What are you in here for?" He looked at me through red swollen eyes and said, "Appendicitis, how about you?" And I replied, "Yes, me too".' He looked at the ground and paused for a moment.

'You know, I really liked this guy, but do you think I could admit that I was not okay emotionally? I could not tell him I was lost and afraid and tired and confused. I so desperately needed a peer to confide in, but did not know how. I needed help, but could not admit it', he said, seeming as though he could hardly believe it himself.

'I find that speaking about emotions is a confronting issue for many men I work with who are your age', I assured him.

He smiled warmly at me and then as if he had come out of a personal trance his television persona took over again. He sincerely wished me well in the future, requesting that I come on his show again when my next book came out.

It was when flying home that it occurred to me that people did not have to come from abusive, dysfunctional backgrounds to be emotionally unfit. It was almost a way of living in the generation of my parents – emotions were not discussed freely, especially by men. Admitting to needing help emotionally was a shameful thing, self-indulgent and weak.

People were emotionally unavailable because they were not emotionally educated. My shrink has been an emotional educator or personal trainer for me and has taught me the things my parents could not teach me because their parents could not teach them. Blame is futile. We are all products of what our parents were able to pass on to us, the assets and the liabilities.

I thought to myself how glad I was that I was living in an age where humanity is evolving emotionally. For I look back on times when there was slavery and women were not allowed to vote and think of it as archaic and ignorant. But people were just not aware. They needed to be educated and informed, and to open their minds and hearts.

I believe there will be a day when emotional fitness becomes as important as physical fitness, a way of life for all males and females, when there will be emotional fitness classes in schools, just like physical fitness is a component of education.

I used to think that there were really screwed-up people like me and normal people. I have come to learn that that was a sort of reverse emotional snobbery. For there are no normal people – I believe that most people spend the second half of their lives getting over the first.

I love that anonymous saying I mentioned earlier in this chapter: 'The only normal people you know are the people you don't know very well.'

Workout **24**
Understanding emotionally unavailable people

I will remember today that not everyone I encounter will be emotionally available and sensitive to my needs. This is a fact of life for everyone. The only way I can help another become emotionally available is to lead by example. Demanding or dictating that another open up to me will only make them feel inadequate and frustrate me.

People open up when they feel safe and they choose to. Most people remain emotionally distant because they have found that it is safer. They have been wounded in the past and use emotional unavailability as a form of protection. Wounds do heal, however, with love and gentleness. People just need time and patience.

However, if I am looking for an intimate relationship with someone who is emotionally unavailable, I must be honest with myself and look at my own motives. Perhaps I am the one who is afraid of emotional involvement, so choosing someone who is emotionally unavailable keeps me safe, for I can focus on them, not myself.

People who are married or emotionally committed to someone else, heavy drinkers, drug takers, workaholics, exercise junkies, gamblers or credit card addicts, overeaters or anorexics, 'cleanaholics' are all focused on an obsession that distracts them from self. These people will not be able to give their emotional truth to me while they are hiding from themselves.

Emotionally unavailable people are not less than emotionally available people; they are just in a different phase of their lives.

For my emotional health today it is best to:
Live and let live, do no harm and mind my own emotional business.

25. Conserving emotional fuel

I gave in to exhaustion. I had such a great time.

Suzanne

'You seem a bit flat, Cynthia. Are you okay?' Sarah asked with gentle concern as we dodged the busy inner-city traffic.

I was driving with my phone earpiece in my ear, eating some dried fruit and nuts that were in my lap, and had one eye on the road as I fumbled for a cassette to insert into the tape player.

'Yeah, I'm fine. I'm good. Why do you ask? I mean, I am busy with having to get the manuscript finished and down to Sydney and run the pilot program and stuff, but yes I feel fine. I'm okay.' I felt a dull sense of panic at her question.

'Well, it's just that your birthday is in a few days, and I just wondered if you were feeling okay', she explained, knowing how emotionally fragile I get every year around the time of my birthday.

I was born on my mother's twenty-first birthday and every year of my life since I was born it was always our birthday. I felt so much guilt throughout my childhood because I had inconvenienced my mother and been born on her birthday. She always went out of her way to make sure I had wonderful parties, with pretty dolly cakes for each girl and Humpty Dumpty cakes for each boy, but it was all too much for me. I always wanted to disappear on my birthday, and when I discovered drugs and alcohol in later life I did disappear emotionally; I became totally numb and pretended I loved our birthday.

My childhood birthday parties were often held in the next-door neighbour's garage. I always hated them. But I would sit there with my hair perfectly curled, my birthday dress on, frilly white socks and patent black leather shoes, and have to smile. The next-door neighbour didn't keep his hands to himself throughout the day. I just wanted to run away. And I also knew what the night ahead held. Mum would be so tired from organising my perfect birthday party that Dad would either bring home alcohol or take her out. This meant that I would either be babysat by the next-door neighbour and abused again on my birthday or Dad would do it after Mum had become intoxicated. I hated birthdays, Mothers' Days, Fathers' Days, Easter and Christmas – in fact, any family celebration day.

Since I had been in recovery and had set my boundaries and started writing and speaking about my life's secrets, my relationship with Mum had become very strained. We no longer spent birthdays together, at my request. I just wanted to be left alone – no cake, no singing, no guilt for being born on her birthday, no fuss – just left alone.

Barbara, Brad, Prue and Sarah all knew this. I just wanted the day to come and go, for it demanded so much emotional fuel to even endure the decades of memories that surfaced on this day.

Sarah knew me very well. She was sensitive to my emotional energy. She was right, I was feeling flat. But more accurately I was feeling overwhelmed by a feeling of impending dread.

I often advised others when they were coping with anniversaries that represented difficult emotional times, such as the death of a loved one, the end of a relationship, birthdays, Christmas and the like, to be gentle with themselves and to slow down and feel the feelings – to be present to themselves and not to take more emotional fuel out of their heart's tank than they had.

I stressed the importance of actually doing less around these emotionally demanding times because to endure them one needs a great deal of fuel in reserve. And if it is not conserved, one can easily crash emotionally.

I suppose it was a little bit of arrogance on my part. I had been in recovery for eight years and each year I hoped that my birthday would get easier. But the reverse seemed to be true. The longer I was in recovery the less denial I had to protect me from my truth. It was as though everything kept becoming clearer each year. More memories surfaced and along with them more pain.

Mal reassured me that my memories were finite and there would come a time when the pain and grief would eventually cease, the wounds would heal and the emotional scar tissue would form. But I was not there yet.

Eight years of recovery work to heal 33 years of denial – no wonder I still had some more work to do.

My birthday fell on a Saturday. The boys had gone to Joe's that weekend and I was glad. If I was going to fall apart I preferred to do it, and let my pain out and be coming through the other side by the time they came home.

I went to bed at 6.30 p.m. on the Friday night, the eve of my birthday. I knew Brad was coming home with my favourite Thai food and almond Magnum ice creams. Brad being nice to me just made me want to retreat. Old feelings of being a burden started to surface. I was in bed when he came home; he came in to see me.

'Gorgie, I have brought you some yummy dinner. Are you going to get up?' he gently asked. Gorgie was his name for me; it was short for 'gorgeous'. He was concerned.

'No, I need to sleep', I answered grudgingly and rolled away from him.

I did not need to sleep; I was hiding from myself, from my emotions. Drugs and alcohol were no longer options, so self-deprivation and sleep as an escape mechanism were my alternatives.

I awoke the next morning still sad and detoxing from old feelings of being a burden, coupled with anxiety that something horrible would happen to me today, as it always used to as a child.

It was the tears in Brad's eyes when he saw my pain that helped me out of bed. I had no energy all day; I was completely drained.

I would remember next year to conserve my emotional fuel in the week preceding my birthday. My own advice is always the hardest to take.

◎ Workout **25**

Conserving emotional fuel

As a car has a specific capacity to store petrol I too have a specific capacity to store emotional energy. A car cannot run indefinitely without refuelling nor can I give out endless amounts of emotional energy without grinding to a sudden halt – especially around demanding emotional anniversaries or events.

◎ ◎ ◎ ◎ ◎

Illness and accidents can sometimes be the result of not listening to my emotional energy tank and not slowing down and refuelling when the alarm light comes on.

◎ ◎ ◎ ◎ ◎

Recovery circles have been using the H.A.L.T. system for years: H stands for Hunger, A is for Anger, L stands for Loneliness and T is for Tired. I can use this, too, as a reminder to listen to my inner alarm system that will warn me when I am almost out of emotional fuel. Whenever I feel hungry, angry, lonely or tired, it is my body telling me to stop what I am doing and refuel or I will burn out. If I go too long without food, I will become irritable and lose momentum; if I get angry and don't deal with it, I will do harm to those around me; if I get lonely and spend too much time away from those I love, I will lose what matters most to me; and if I don't get the specific amount of sleep my body needs to refill my emotional tank, I will be ineffective and not enjoy my day.

◎ ◎ ◎ ◎ ◎

I can conserve my emotional energy today by remembering:

I can say no to others … I am not a robot … It is my responsibility to look after my own needs … I need to feel my feelings, not hide from them, but I don't have to do this alone.

26. Freedom from worrying about what others think

Freedom is what you do with what's been done to you.

Jean-Paul Sartre

There were two television camera crews standing in front of me and four microphones held at my mouth asking for comments on the issue of abused children and what happens to them if they don't get help.

As a top ten bestselling author I was now often asked by the media for comment on the issues I had written about in my first book. I relished the opportunity to be useful.

I was doing a keynote address on this beautiful spring morning to raise awareness of the Abused Child Trust – a non-profit organisation I felt proud to represent. I was standing in the playground where abused preschool children aged between three and five were playing under the care of special counsellors and therapists. I felt thunder in my heart around these wounded little people and a great sense of responsibility to speak the truth, gently, but without editing the socially unacceptable bits.

'Well, I was one of these children that did not get help as a child. I lost nineteen years of my life to drug and alcohol addiction and eating disorders. I lied, I cheated, I stole and I prostituted my body. I never worked as a sex worker, but there were nights when I was on the streets as a teenager that I had sex with strangers for somewhere to sleep. It was easier to have sex with someone I did not know than to remain in the denial and insanity of my father's or mother's home. I stole from society because I felt society had stolen from me, and I lied because I had no tools to cope with my truth. It is no wonder that 85 percent of our prisons are filled with people who were abused as children – it makes you angry, but of course that is no excuse not to heal', I explained, focusing on the eyes of the interviewers so that I did not become overwhelmed by the fact that I was speaking to a few million people who would be watching the nightly news on these two high rating TV channels that evening.

The cameramen thanked me for my honesty and the interviewers asked for my business card. I felt pleased that my morning had started out so productively. I had a huge day ahead – a support group to run and three meetings to squeeze in before picking up Sam from rugby training, dropping him home and getting dinner organised for the boys, and then going out and giving another keynote address at 7 p.m. that evening.

The day rushed past and as I prepared for the evening ahead, putting on my corporate red dress, I assured myself that I would be fine addressing a room full of starchy academics. The dress was a wonderful fit and the colour itself was empowering. Having left school so young and not having any formal education, addressing highly educated people was always a challenge to my self-worth.

Dinner was in the oven when I decided to turn on the 6 o'clock news to see if any of my interviews were being shown.

'Mum might be on the news tonight, boys. I did an interview for the Abused Child Trust today. Do you want to watch?' I asked, pleased with myself that I felt I was on my way to raising awareness about this difficult subject.

'Sure, what channel?' Mitch said as he grabbed the remote control. Just getting to hold the remote control in my house was a feat in itself.

Mitch nestled in close to me and put his head on my shoulder. I loved his boyish smell. Sam sat on the other side of me as we watched the news begin.

The feature stories of the day played for the first ten minutes and I was about to get up when I heard the newsreader say:

'At the Abused Child Trust launch today Cynthia Morton, prostitute, said …' My heart went cold.

After all the things I had achieved with my book and my public speaking, they chose not to introduce me as an author or even as a survivor, but as a prostitute. I immediately thought of the boys. All their mates at school knew I was Sam and Mitchell's mother. And I had just been called a hooker on the nightly news.

'Boys, I am so sorry that they called me that. You know that they have taken my teenage years out of context. I am so very sorry you had to hear that', I said with tears in my throat.

Mitchell said nothing but just wrapped his arms around me very reassuringly.

'Mum, it's just media crap. Don't worry about it. We learn about it at school – they just have to sensationalise everything. We know who you are, and we are proud of you', Sam said firmly with a note of annoyance in his voice at the TV station.

It seemed ironic that the same television channel just a year before had decided that my title was 'An Australian Hero' and now a year later they had decided that my new title was 'A Prostitute'. I was coming to understand that the media could be your best friend or your worst enemy and that it depended upon the integrity of the person doing the story and the heading that was going to sell.

Another large, glossy fashion magazine had also interviewed me earlier that year. They wanted a feature on myself and my journey, including a photograph of the boys and me.

The journalist seemed like a wonderful person, and as she asked me questions I reminded her that my children had to be able to read this so their feelings were to be considered when she put the story together. She assured me that she was thrilled to tell my story and would be sensitive to the boys.

I told her about my suicidal times, when driving off a bridge seemed one of my only options, but I also told her how my love for the boys was what drove me to get help.

When the article hit the newsstands nationally, it was titled, 'The day I nearly killed my children'.

Another leading Brisbane journalist writing for a newspaper asked me about my mother and my childhood. I remember saying to her: 'My mother was a battered woman; there was not a lot she could do. She has her own issues that she chooses not to look at, but please respect my mother – she could well read this, so just leave her out of it.'

'No problem, Cynthia, it's off the record', she assured me.

Of course, when the newspaper article came out, it read: 'Her mother was of no use, as a battered woman.'

It was becoming increasingly difficult to tell my story in its entirety without others being misrepresented or me being misquoted. I was starting to understand that probably everything I read in magazines about other people was maybe 50–60 percent accurate – at best. My boys consistently became annoyed that their ages and other dates and details were printed back to front or were just completely wrong.

Not worrying about others' opinions of me was something I was beginning to get a lot of emotional homework on. But the media's opinion of me and the opinions of people who read magazine and newspaper articles I cannot control.

I had another test one morning as I sat and waited for my shrink to call me in for my appointment. I was sitting in the waiting room with everyone else, arrogantly thinking to myself that I was probably the sanest person there. I was wearing a very comfortable, loose-fitting summer dress. It had thin shoulder straps and just fell to my ankles hardly touching my body. It was very cool on hot summer days.

'I love your dress. You look so willowy and slender in it that I just had to tell you', a young girl who had just been called into her appointment said as she walked past me.

'Thank you', I said. I did love this dress, too, and even more now that I seemed to look willowy and slender in it.

Just then, a man in his late thirties walked into the reception area and sat next to me. I got up to get a magazine and moved one seat away. I needed space.

'When's your baby due?' he asked genuinely with a smile.

'I'm not pregnant', I said firmly as I raised the magazine to eye level so I did not have to look at him.

I had gone from being complimented on my slender figure to being asked if I was pregnant, even though I was wearing the same dress, in the space of two minutes. I was able to smile to myself as I realised that people's opinions are so varied that it's a waste of energy worrying about them.

That night I left the boys at home as they had reassured me they were fine following the hooker comment on the news. As I drove into the plush hotel I hoped that most people would have been making their way to this event and would not have had time to have seen the news. It was only that I lived five minutes from the inner city that I had had time to see it.

I was seated at the VIP table with all the esteemed guests and academics. I took a deep breath and smiled as I took my seat. The floral centrepiece was beautiful and the menu placed in front of me looked superb. About 200 people had gathered at this event to hear me speak. The hooker on tonight's news! Hopefully nobody saw it.

'I saw you on the news tonight, dear, and I am really looking forward to hearing you speak', the woman next to me said as she nudged me and gave me a wink.

I laughed.

◎ Workout 26

Freedom from worrying about what others think

Worrying about what other people think of me is like trying to empty the ocean with a teaspoon – it is a futile exercise!

◎ ◎ ◎ ◎ ◎

People change their minds in a second and those who have once disliked me can often turn around in later years to be my greatest admirers. And the reverse is also true: those who have loved and supported me can change their minds and choose to move away. I cannot control the choices of another, so why try?

◎ ◎ ◎ ◎ ◎

The saying 'What other people think of me is none of my business' is an important but sometimes difficult sentiment to digest. What goes on in my mind is no-one else's business, as what goes on in the minds of others is not my business. Trying to control and maintain control of what others think takes me away from the here and now.

Focusing on what others think removes the focus from my
internal viewpoint and the most important relationship I will
ever have – the one with myself. What I think about my own
thoughts, feelings, words and actions is where my self-worth is
built. To respect who I am and like and approve of all of my
thoughts, feelings, words and actions is a huge task today.

I will mind my own business today by:

- not scanning others for fault
- avoiding those who gossip
- focusing on not invading others' privacy with my thoughts
- not judging passers-by for entertainment
- remembering that different from me does not automatically
  mean wrong
- remembering to live and let live.

27. Deserving success, money and recognition

If I denied my potential I felt I was being loyal to my father, helping him cope – as he needed to believe I was not intelligent so he felt safer abusing me. But long after he died, as an adult woman, I felt I was betraying him if I dared to achieve.

Cynthia Morton

'Cynthia, we can only pay you what we are paying the other speaker – $1000 per day plus expenses. Is that acceptable?' the voice on the other end of the phone enquired.

I was being asked to go to northern New South Wales to the small coastal town of Ballina to speak to five different schools in the area. I would be doing a tour with another speaker who was a national radio personality and an expert on addiction. He had his own radio spot and was an academic.

'Yes, that's fine, I am available and I would love to do it', I replied, gobsmacked at the invitation and the offer to be paid such a huge amount.

It was the first speaking engagement for which I had been offered that amount of money. Over the past year since my book had come out I had spoken mostly for charities that had no budget for speakers. Nonetheless, I was often overwhelmed by the standing ovations I received and sometimes became a little confused as to what I had said that was deserving of such a fantastic response. But there was a nagging feeling in my throat about this engagement. I was afraid – and couldn't work out why.

I drove to Ballina a month or so later, surprised that it hadn't been cancelled. It had seemed like a too-good-to-be-true sort of offer.

I sang to myself the whole way. This was always good therapy and helped me to stop thinking about the forthcoming event and to stay present to the moment. I did not know all the words, but I sang my heart out to this new song about letting yourself shine. It seemed as if it had been written for me.

Giving myself permission to shine – to be seen – was such hard work for me, without feeling guilty or unworthy. And to be paid at the same time – wow, I could not believe it.

My little hotel room was a delight. I unpacked the car. I had brought far more clothes and shoes than I needed, but I liked to have a choice so that I could dress to suit how I felt before I had to speak. I ordered steak and salad through room service, put on my white, fluffy shower robe and navigated the remote control. I knew I had an early radio interview to do before the five schools the following day, so I ate dinner and rang Brad and the boys before turning off the light at 9 p.m.

The next morning I decided on the pink jacket and black pants and top. I always brought other options but usually went with the pink. I understood Julia Roberts in that movie where she said 'Pink is my signature colour' in a deep southern accent. It was my signature colour too. It always felt right.

The radio interview went well. I felt invigorated and ready to go. My heart was pumping; God, I loved feeling useful.

The organisers picked me up at the designated time, and the other speaker and I made our way around the five schools.

At every event, a few students would approach me afterwards with tear-filled eyes, as I had just told their story. Pain is such a universal language. We were complete strangers, but I would hold my arms out and hug them and we would just stand there like two passengers that had survived a shipwreck years ago and had just bumped into each other again. These young people sobbing on my pink jacket were an honour to hold – so beautiful, so young and so brave to be able to feel their pain. I had been too afraid to acknowledge my wounding at their age. We swapped email addresses and deep pupil contact and knew that all would be well as long as we had others who understood.

That Buddhist saying, 'We are all alone – together', always comes to mind at times such as this.

As I began the two-and-a-half-hour drive back to Brisbane I felt privileged to have met all those young students and to have had the opportunity to let them know that I was coming back from a journey many of them were beginning to head out on – addiction and self-denial. And I wished that I had had someone speak to me at their age to explain that the journey is far too expensive for the soul and that only 3–5 percent ever make it back alive.

I placed my plastic bag full of mixed nuts and fruit between my thighs to nibble on the journey home. My water bottle was in its holder, my favourite cassette tapes sorted for easy access as I drove and my mobile phone earpiece was in my ear. I loved to drive alone; it was a good time to just be with me.

As I crossed the Tweed Heads border that divides Queensland and New South Wales tears began to well in my eyes. The countryside and the ocean views were stunning, but it was more than Mother Nature's landscape. I felt overwhelmed with grief. Heavy, hot tears started to fill my eyes and the huge lump in my throat became painful.

A really old Eighties' tape had found its way into the player and a ballad called 'In the Living Years' started to play. It was about the singer not saying what he needed to say to his father before his father died. My dad's image began to appear before my eyes – almost as if his face was looking back at me through the windscreen. I immediately felt like I was in trouble – like I had betrayed him. How could somebody with poor learning ability at school, who was known as a child for being silly and clumsy, be paid $1000 per day to speak their truth – to be an equal with an academic?

It meant my dad was wrong about me. I had always known it but had kept quiet about it. He had been dead nearly seventeen years and with each passing year I dared to access more of my potential. But it felt like this time I had gone too far and that I was in trouble with him.

I sobbed all the way home, feeling deep grief as if someone had just died. It felt like I had just been to a funeral. And I had – it was the death of the need for my father's approval.

Later the following week I was conducting a workshop with some fellow facilitators who worked with survivors and addicts alongside me. I told Peter and Tim, two men I felt safe with, that I wanted to do some work around my father – I needed to have a dialogue with him; I had unspoken words I needed to say.

'The Unsaid' was an exercise we often did with those who had issues with people in their past who were either dead or emotionally unsafe to be in contact with. It was a powerful way to release unfinished emotional business.

Tim and Peter were both big men in stature who had a genuine caring relationship with me. They were fellow travellers who had no sexual agenda; they were not predators, but safe gentlemen with integrity.

'Tim, can you and Peter both sit facing me? We'll put a chair behind you both, but facing me, where I will put my father. I know it sounds crazy, but if he went to physically attack me I know you could both stop him. He scares the shit out of me still and I know that what I need to say to him will make him mad', I said with tears in my eyes.

'No problems, sweetheart, he won't get near you. We won't let him hurt you, you are safe now', Tim said, looking directly at me with his deep chocolate eyes. Tim was an ex-SAS Marine whose shaved head and pierced ear could be intimidating if you did not know his heart.

We took up our positions, and I put my head in my hands. I brought to my mind's eye the image of Pam, the Black Panther. She had shown up in my morning meditation that day. Pam had been lurking in my subconscious for years. I first met her at the end of my using. I recall lying in bed in the early hours one morning, extremely sick from the vomiting and drug and alcohol abuse the night before. I had just been to the toilet and had returned to bed, and I was wide awake when I first felt her.

We lived down an easement block with a very long driveway. I could feel and visualise Pam stalking our driveway. She was huge, larger than our whole house, and her coat was so shiny and black that it reflected the colour blue. She was looking for me. I felt the earth shake and closed my eyes certain that she would take our roof off with one swipe and pick me up with a paw and eat me with just one mouthful. Instead, I felt her pace around the house and as I felt her walk past our bedroom I closed my eyes, too terrified to see her. Then she proceeded back up the driveway and left. It was almost as if her only purpose was to make her presence known to me.

I put the experience down to too many drugs and never thought of it again until the following year when I was clean and sober. I had begun meditating in the mornings, bringing up visions of little Cynthia aged around four. I just needed to remember the pure little girl I once was who deserved to be protected and treated with dignity. I would bring up a vision of her and carry that vision with me all day. Any time I thought or spoke offensively towards myself, I would ask myself the question, 'Would I speak to little Cynthia with such hostility?', and the answer was always no.

Then beautiful huge animals started showing up in my morning meditations. I would be visualising little Cynthia when a beautiful huge elephant with pink bows on her tail and pink peony roses behind her ears introduced herself as Ellie, my guide to female wisdom, or Dulcie, the Pink Dolphin, who I had already met in the Amazon and who brought me relaxation and peace, or Sid, the Silverback Ape, who brought out my Alpha male energy ... the characters kept coming.

Then Pam showed up one morning. She was huge, as I had previously remembered her. She picked me up and put me on her back. Little four-year-old Cynthia got to ride on the back of this huge, powerful panther called Pam for the day. I felt so empowered. Pam was about empowerment. Taja and Toro, a male and female tiger duo, also showed up. They showed me how to self-preserve and protect my territory. The list of my other guides would make another book.

My shrink had described Pam as a message from my subconscious calling me to wake up while I was using. For in those days I was too afraid of my personal power to straddle it. But things were different now.

Anyway, Pam had shown up in my morning meditation that day. I didn't really like it when she showed up because history had revealed that I really needed to extend myself emotionally on the days she appeared, so I was always a little concerned that it was going to be a challenging day ahead. This day proved to be no different.

'Dad, I need to talk to you', I said, looking at the empty chair behind Tim and Peter. A part of me felt stupid speaking to an imaginary chair, but I had witnessed many people having huge breakthroughs by allowing themselves the opportunity to speak their truth. I knew it worked. I wanted to be free from my father.

As I had talked others through this exercise, I knew I had to visualise my father – what he would be wearing, his face, his expressions – so I did. He was wearing a camel-coloured cardigan that he often used to wear. His face, a Charles Bronson type of face, craggy, tanned but hand-some, with angry eyebrows, looked back at me. He was a physically strong man, but not very tall, perhaps 178 centimetres.

I could see Dad now, looking back at me. He was angry and doing his best to intimidate me back to a state of silence. His violence always resulted in my silence. I could see his dead crocodile eyes and could remember the fear they instilled in me as a little girl. But today it would be different. I had no need to be afraid. I had backup – Tim, Peter and Pam.

Dead Crocodile Eyes

A heavy pick axe, his body feels like cold lead
No mercy, he is too strong, I wish either he or I were dead
His eyes like a crocodile's – don't focus, only stare
My daddy leaves his body, he is no longer there

The Croc talks to voices that hurt him when he was small
I am still and silent staring frozen at the wall
I try so hard to be brave, he knows I won't tell
It hurts so much, but I have learned how not to yell

When he cries I can love him for on his cheek I see a tear
I feel special when he hugs me 'cos we both know so much fear
In the morning he is angry and doesn't want me in his sight
He knows I remember what he did to me last night

My peas spill off my dinner plate as I nervously eat my food
He knocks me off my chair; it's my fault he's in a bad mood
I am silly and clumsy and not very smart
Not really good at anything except playing Barbies and doing art

I have learned about danger, I detect it through smell and the eyes
Now a woman I know crocodiles no matter how well they disguise
Sometimes they smile and offer you a pretty decoy
But the eyes say so much more …
Today I am nobody's toy.

I looked to the floor and started to cry.

'Dad, I was never dumb. I used to act dumb because I knew you needed to believe that I was. You needed to believe I was terrified of you, and most of the time I was. Your beatings did hurt. But Dad, you were wrong about me. I am smart. I can do things. I have stuff I want to say and words I need to write', I tried to look up at him but I was too afraid. I knew he could hear me, I just couldn't face him.

'Look him in the eye, love, you are strong enough. Say it to his face – he's a coward, he always was, he knows he can't get to you with us here. Be the woman you are and say it to his face.' Tim's voice was filled with compassion. 'Come on, sweetheart, it's time.'

I placed a finger each side of my eyes and pulled them back as if I was a cat, and I looked up and straight at him.

'Dad, I love you, but you are on your own now. I have to go my own way. I cannot pretend for you any more. I need to leave you because to stay with you I have to pretend for you. I was paid that money, Dad, because I deserve it. I work hard, I try hard, and I am going to keep going and not be afraid to be a success on every level. I can't hold myself back for you any more, Dad. I love you, but I have to go ...' I really started to cry and looked down again.

'Say goodbye to him, Cynthia, let him go', Tim urged.

My tear-filled eyes could hardly open. 'I can't leave him, Tim, he needs me, he's afraid.'

'Let him go, love, say goodbye, you can do it. It's time now.'

I closed my eyes and felt Pam's strength rise inside me.

I looked straight at this man who used to terrify me. I was suddenly filled with a strong sense of peace and safety.

'Goodbye, Dad, I'll see you on the other side – and thank you.'

◎ Workout 27

Deserving success, money and recognition

As Nelson Mandela so beautifully put it, 'You are a child of the Universe, your playing small doesn't serve the world, there is nothing enlightened about shrinking and hiding so that people don't feel insecure around you … as we are liberated from our own fear our presence automatically liberates others.'

◎ ◎ ◎ ◎ ◎

I choose to remember those words of wisdom today. The main emotion that prevents me from enjoying money, recognition and success is guilt that is born from worrying about other people's opinions and looking for their approval instead of my own.

◎ ◎ ◎ ◎ ◎

I will remember that money is merely an exchange of energy; it has no power other than what I give it. I give myself permission to enjoy any money I earn – to spend, to save or to donate it is my choice.

◎ ◎ ◎ ◎ ◎

I give myself permission to be recognised for my talents and potential. I will remember that my talents do not make me less or more than anyone else, simply different. I am allowed to smile and say thank you when someone recognises my worth. I will not negate their compliment and throw it back at them.

◎ ◎ ◎ ◎ ◎

I measure my success by the peace of mind in my head and heart. If I can look into my own pupils today and sincerely smile back at the person I have become and also look at my naked body in the mirror with gratitude for the years of loyal service it has provided for me – then I am a true success.

◎ ◎ ◎ ◎ ◎

I will remember today when it comes to money, recognition or success that:

I am worthy … I deserve this … I can relax.

28. Trusting in trust

Until you can trust yourself to be true to your own heart, you
will be unable to trust another.

Cynthia Morton

'We would love to do a national exclusive. Please don't do any television media until we do ours. It won't be until the New Year as things are winding down now, but we will do your story. Thank you for contacting us', she said as she hung up the phone.

I was stunned. In all my wildest dreams, I had never expected this show to phone me. It was too good to be true. I so wanted this television station to feature our work. It was national and the highest-rating show of its type in Australia. It was my first choice. Even though I had sent our award-winning video to many television stations, they were the first to respond. I could not believe it. Other shows called me after their call, wanting to tell our story, but I told them all I had agreed to an exclusive. And every time I said it a shudder of excitement went through me.

I had to run outside to where the group was having a cigarette break in the sun to tell them the news.

'Guess who is doing our story, guess who wants an exclusive?' I taunted as everyone looked up, smiling at me.

I told them proudly. 'They want us, a feature story on our Emotional Fitness program, our little award-winning documentary about us!' I was jumping up and down now. I could not stop smiling; it was our long-awaited breakthrough. We all had worked so hard – we deserved this.

The others were hugging me and each other, dancing and smiling and shouting 'Yes!' as they punched the air with their fists. They were all amazing human beings and had all worked on the pilot program with me. They had opened their hearts and bared their souls in the hope that our little documentary would help others.

Our documentary was entered into a national competition for Australian documentary makers. It was up against other professional documentaries about Tibetan monks and other amazing stories filmed in exotic locations with huge budgets. But we won, we won first prize. A group of recovering drug addicts, alcoholics, sex workers and society's supposed no-hopers – our story won. And now the whole of Australia would hear about our work and hopefully we could attract some sponsorship and funding so we could continue helping others around the nation.

The New Year came and went and I touched base with the 'exclusive' TV program in February 2003, giving them January to catch their breath.

'We are still very interested, leave it with me, I will be in touch soon', she assured me as my heart pounded, hoping I hadn't dreamt the whole thing up.

By April I had a meeting in Sydney with a potential publisher for this book you are now reading, so I phoned the Supervising Producer again.

'Hi, I will be down in Sydney meeting with a publisher next week. I can drop in and have a chat about the story if it suits you', I said, trying not to sound too desperate for some feedback.

'Sure, that sounds great, call me when you arrive and I will make some time in the day for you', she responded, still sounding interested.

I arrived and phoned her from the taxi as I made my way to meet my potential publisher. We organised a meeting for 2 p.m., which would give me enough time to explain my ideas and concepts to the publisher, have some lunch and then meet up with her.

The taxi pulled up near the security gate outside the TV station. I gave the driver the producer's name and I was given a security tag to wear.

As soon as I met her I knew in my gut that she had a resistance to me. I don't know if it was because of the way I looked or what it was. I just felt it. The meeting went well though. She asked me lots of pointed questions – it felt like a test – but I answered every one. She did not rattle me at all and maybe that was the problem. She discussed who she would like to have tell the story. The journalists on the program are all famous in their own right, but I did not agree with the one she chose. I felt that one woman journalist, in particular, would really 'get' what we were about from having seen previous interviews she had done. But she was the boss so I gently expressed my opinion, feeling straightaway that it was not appreciated.

She promised to be in touch within a few weeks to get things underway.

A month passed before I called again. She did not return my call. So I emailed her. Two days later she replied, saying that due to the war in Iraq, the program did not have the staff available to send to Brisbane now or in the foreseeable future. So they would not be able to feature our story.

I understood that the war had monopolised current affairs programs over the past months, but I knew her excuse was not well founded. In the months that followed there were several stories that were filmed in Brisbane.

For some reason she had lost interest.

Being told one thing but knowing that there was an undercurrent that contradicted what I was being told was all too familiar to me. I so wanted to trust in people, and in their words. What upset me more than anything was that the whole group had been holding onto her words for the past eight months, trusting she would honour them, not just me.

As a child and when I first came into recovery I used to believe that nobody was trustworthy because I did not trust myself. I was now learning to trust myself and, when it felt right, to trust others.

I knew when I met this woman that there was resistance. That knowing I can trust. But I chose to ignore it because I did not want it to be true. My truth did not suit me.

My truth was often inconvenient but I knew that just because she had let me down it was not a reason to give up. I could still trust in my dream and in the power of our work.

Brad summed it up beautifully for me that evening as I sat and cried in disappointment.

'Gorgie, you've got to be careful who you put your trust in. And the media is probably not the safest industry to trust. You know that by now with all the interviews you've done where you've been misquoted or exaggerated. But don't taint everyone with the same brush. The best thing with new people you meet is to go with your gut, and if you are unsure whether you trust them, wait and see. People have to earn trust. Don't automatically give it. Listen to your truth, sweetheart; I hate to see you put yourself through this. It will happen, I believe in you', he comforted me as I cried.

I believe in me now, too, and with belief comes trust – I could trust myself to carry on. Years ago someone letting me down would have knocked me over emotionally for days. Nowadays it was only hours – I was making progress with understanding and trusting trust.

Workout **28**

Trusting in trust

Trust without belief is an impossible task. If I do not believe in someone or something, I now understand that I will not know trust.

If I cannot believe in myself and my own ability, another person, love, nature, science, a god, an animal or life itself, then how can I trust anything or anyone? To believe in something or someone is to underwrite it or them with the deepest part of myself. If I am unable to access the deepest part of myself – my heart and my soul – then I am destined to live a superficial life. If I am partaking in emotionally numbing substances my ability to find trust will be sabotaged. Drugs, pills, alcohol, unresolved childhood trauma and eating disorders are trust killers. My relationship with myself is where trust is born. Can I look at a photograph of myself as a child and see beauty and love? Can I look at other children and see potential and hope?

Can I trust trust? If my trust has been abused it can be difficult to trust that trust is trustworthy. I will be patient with myself today if trust is a difficult task for me. Trust is not an automatic reflex; it is built over time. It can be destroyed, but it can also be rebuilt with time and patience. Some humans – emotional sharks – are untrustworthy; others – emotional dolphins – are trustworthy. Just because I have been wounded by a shark it does not mean that everyone with a grey fin is a shark.

Dolphins do exist. Am I living with tunnel vision in order to protect myself from being hurt? Pain is often more about expectation than actual events.

◎ ◎ ◎ ◎ ◎

Fear and unrealistic expectations will destroy my ability to trust today. I can slowly allow myself to trust my own heart and the belief that I am deserving.

◎ ◎ ◎ ◎ ◎

It is safe to trust. I can start by trusting myself:
I will start with baby steps ... I can trust myself to accept that I am not perfect ... I can trust that each day holds new opportunities for me ... I am the only person holding me back today – I can use the past to help create a better future.

29. Controlling my need to control

The size of your body is of little account;
The size of your brain is of much account;
The size of your heart is of the most account of all.

B C Forbes

'You'll end up the size of a house', my mother would say with fear in her voice as I stood in the kitchen as a teenager eating two chocolate biscuits.

I had watched Mum chain-smoke, drink strong, black coffee without sugar, take laxatives and have many a liquid lunch consisting mainly of cheap cask wine all her life in order to keep her figure. And it was a slim figure – her methods worked. She was so much smaller than me in height – at least 13 centimetres. I never felt like her daughter; I felt like an elephant next to her.

As I grew from a teenager into a woman, how much I weighed and what size my clothes were became the measure of my self-esteem – up until a short time ago, as a middle-aged woman.

It was almost as if when I was starving and obsessed with my figure I was being a good girl, loyal to Mum, living by her yardstick, helping her feel safe. She did not like fat on herself or her daughters. Whenever my mother met another woman she would always comment on her figure and her hair once the woman had left the room. That was how she measured their worth and her own.

I had learnt at a very young age that my hair was basically a write-off. It was too thin – shocking hair, like string, as my grandmother used to put it. Whenever my grandmother came to visit it became obvious where Mum had picked up her habits.

'Cindy, your tummy's big, you've put on weight', Grandma would say with a note of delight in her voice. It did not matter if I had given birth a few months earlier, she was ever critical of how I looked and always had a negative comment about my body or my hair.

Over the years, I had starved and binged, my weight ranging from 59 kilograms at the end of my addictions to 97 kilograms during my pregnancies. It was only when I was pregnant that I would give myself permission to eat without guilt. While I remained abstinent from drugs and alcohol, I replaced them with a more sociably acceptable drug, high sugar and high fat foods.

I had been in recovery for eight years. When I began my recovery in 1995 I weighed 59 kilograms. At age 41 I was 72 kilograms and living in an emotional gaol when it came to body image. Any love I had for my body was what I called 'lemon juice love'.

Lemon Juice Love

Fine paper cuts on my fingertips that no-one can see
As my hands are forced into lemon juice, please let me be
They want to soothe me and comfort but I want to push them away
Love stings, I don't want their comfort but that I must not say

They don't want me to cry, I must keep secrets, nothing to tell
They all look so perfect and happy but I just want to yell
Get me out of here, I don't like people, I want to fly away
The sparrows are my only buddies, they visit me every day

Well how about a biscuit, chocolate or some creamy cake?
I have learned it temporarily numbs the pain; I love it when she bakes
Feelings are too painful; enough food can make them go numb
My small tummy is swollen, pain is buried, give me that last crumb!

My hair is perfect; I look pretty and have frilly white socks
Stop sulking, ungrateful child, go and sit on his knee
I hate my birthday and this life
I want to run away and be free

Behave, don't be silly, and don't you dare cry
Pretending is how one lives ... no it's only a little white lie
Lemon juice love, cold hands with texture like chalk
What is wrong with you child, why won't you talk?

If I was allowed to tell the truth – what would I say?
I want to be dead or just run away
No that's too scary; I would get the wooden spoon
Or a long and hard belting for my own good, then be sent to my room

The violence, the screaming
Thuds on the wall
Block my ears, get under the covers
There is no-one to call

So I eat cake and wince with the lemon juice love
But must be thin and wear jeans that fit like a glove
I can vomit and eat and pretend with the best
I have long buried the truth, I lie with the rest.

I had been working out with a personal trainer five days a week. My arms were as sculpted as Madonna's. I was a size 12, which was not small enough as far as I was concerned. But even when I had been a size 10 I was still not happy.

I had decided that I was gluten intolerant because every time I ate anything with wheat grains I felt full. I told myself that feeling full was bad; in actual fact, it was just uncomfortable because I was more comfortable feeling empty and hungry. That was my natural state – one of constant deprivation. It seemed like I was trapped in this gaol of either deprivation or overcompensation.

I have since come to learn that if any human being goes without gluten for an extended period of time and then suddenly reintroduces it into their diet they will become uncomfortable and have bowel pains, simply because their body has to readjust again. Some people, I understand, are genuinely gluten intolerant but mine was self-imposed – to feel satisfied and full somehow felt wrong.

All my clothes were a little too small for me. I bought them that way as insurance against putting on weight. I had thousands of dollars worth of designer clothes, all just fitting or a little too small.

I had also decided that anything with white sugar, chocolate, or anything that was sweet was not good for me. During my early recovery when I was coming off alcohol and other substances, my body naturally craved sugar as alcohol contains a lot of sugar. I told myself that this was bad for me. If I wanted it and it gave me pleasure then it must be bad for me. I became a tyrant. It felt wrong to give to myself or to allow myself to enjoy pleasure. I was afraid of the overwhelming state of naturally feeling good, as it made me surrender to life. Surrendering my emotional control was my biggest fear because I felt so much about so much that I though my heart would drown me if I let it feel.

It was April 2003 when I decided to do it – to throw away my scales. I had been living without white sugar, cakes and pastries for eighteen months, on a self-imposed gluten-free diet for two years and had not eaten chocolate for five years. It was not about health but about control.

My self-esteem was measured every morning by how much I weighed. Since I had stopped working with my personal trainer I was more obsessed with my weight than I ever had been.

Apart from the huge expense, I had come to see that my personal trainer had become like a drug dealer to me. Each week he would put the bar up higher and I would hurt myself trying to please him, just to get that high, that rush, that approval. It was becoming self-abusive. I was never satisfied with the result in the mirror. I look back at photographs of me at that time and my stomach was like a rock. I was very strong, but I had become an exercise addict.

I had lost the ability to choose whether I went to the gym or not, just as I had lost the ability to choose whether I took drugs or consumed alcohol many years before. People who have balance with drugs, alcohol and exercise do it because they want to. I did it because I had to. Some addictions are biochemical and some are behavioural. I was not sure which category exercise belonged in but there was no doubt that I was out of control and had become a slave to the adrenalin.

My self-esteem was monitored by how long I spent at the gym and how much I tortured myself. I ate less and less because the muscle I was developing was moving the scales upwards, but my clothes' sizes were going down. I was pleased and terrified at the same time. I was in emotional chaos.

As an addict, anything that hits the pleasure centres in my brain can be used to abuse myself. I can use anything that is supposed to bring pleasure and become obsessive – not just drugs, alcohol and now exercise, but sex, work, spending, sleeping, eating or dieting.

I had been in quite a lot of emotional turmoil about my estrangement from my mother since I had been in recovery, so I needed to control my weight to be good. Even though my mother and I did not speak any more, by being a good girl about my weight, I felt as though I was at least honouring her wishes at some level. Intellectually, I knew this was silly, but I had to reach a level of emotional maturity where I was strong enough to let go of her too, just as I had let go of Dad in order to honour my truth about deserving success. And I knew after having worked with thousands of other people in recovery that you are only ready for emotional change when you feel safe enough and strong enough and not before.

I was ready to let go of the need for my mother's approval in my own mind and to discover the natural state of my body when it was not excessively controlled. I did not want to be scared of growing older and softer with time. I so wanted to be a soft grandmother who gave warm hugs and embraced age with grace and dignity.

I had recently seen a photograph of my older sister. She looked more like my mother than ever before – unhealthily thin, much thinner than her daughters as Mum always was. She was a stranger to me. She had perfected the external image but I knew the control that it took to keep up that facade. I knew all the chaos that was going on in her life underneath that perfect family photograph. I felt sad that she was still trapped in having to be the perfect hero child, keeping up appearances as Mum had taught us.

'I just don't want to live my life measuring my self-worth on these scales any more, Barb. They run my life. Every morning I wake up and wonder what they will say, and that dictates what I am and am not allowed to eat during the day. I want to throw them away. I don't know how fat I will get, and I hope Brad will still find me attractive. Do you think it's a good idea, Barb?' I could hear the nonsense I was speaking and knew that I had to stop giving away my power to this metal box of numbers.

'Yes, love, I think it's time. But I don't want you to throw them in the bin outside. Go and find an industrial bin somewhere and dump them, otherwise you'll have them back on the bathroom floor by tonight. Yes, get rid of them, it's time, and about bloody time I must say. You can trust your instincts to help you find your body's balance. They have never let you down before. Go by how you feel, you can trust that. But you might need to be patient. You have been controlling your weight for many years. You may have to give yourself twelve months before your body settles at its natural weight', she said with excitement and relief in her voice.

My heart started to pound. I was afraid to be without my scales, just as I had been afraid to be without drugs, cigarettes and alcohol. In hindsight, giving them up was the most empowering thing I ever did. I knew in my heart that it would be good for me to give them up. But who would I be without them? What shape would I become? I did wonder if Brad would still find me attractive if I was bigger. And I knew that I would get bigger as I had always deprived myself of food so much. I wondered if I would be brave enough to let myself taste chocolate again. And bread – God, to be able to eat a sandwich and not feel that I would be left out of the human race because I was not lovable or acceptable enough as I was not the right size. What freedom!

The most important thing I wanted to know was: would I still be loving towards myself no matter what size I became. It no longer mattered if Mum emotionally abandoned me. We had been apart physically for years and now I was getting ready to leave her emotionally. But the biggest question was: would I abandon myself?

◎ Workout **29**

Controlling my need to control

I will pay attention to my level of frustration today for it is the warning bell that I am out of balance with my need to control. I will remind myself that I cannot control people, places and things, and I will cause myself untold levels of frustration if I will not accept this today.

◎ ◎ ◎ ◎ ◎

I will remember that accidents happen, people forget things, people get sick, die, lie, cheat, change their minds, steal, leave, stay, contradict themselves and act irrationally at times.

◎ ◎ ◎ ◎ ◎

If I become obsessive about my external world, for example, whether the cushions are sitting perfectly on the bed or the washing is hung out in order or the food shopping put away correctly, or if I have to park in the same area at a car park or use the same cubicle in a public toilet, it is sometimes a sign of inner turmoil or emotional chaos. By focusing on the physical, I gain some feeling of control.

◎ ◎ ◎ ◎ ◎

I will also remember that I am offended when others attempt to control me because this means that they do not accept me as I am. If they want me to change my clothes, the way I eat, what I do or don't say, how I act, walk, sleep or merely exist, it is their problem not mine. I will remember that they need to do some acceptance homework. I am open to a gentle request or a statement of preference but not a demand, so I will not give out today what I do not like to receive.

◎ ◎ ◎ ◎ ◎

I can identify controlling behaviour today through these key words:

Don't do ... Don't say ... Don't come ... Don't go ... Don't be ... You should ... You shouldn't ...

30. Accepting acceptance

To love oneself is the beginning of a lifelong romance.

Oscar Wilde

Six months have passed since I threw away my scales. I feel like I am free-falling. I have no idea how I much I weigh, and with each passing day it matters less and less.

Like the true addict I am, the only way I could get through my fear during the first few weeks was to tell myself that I would go and buy another set of scales at the end of the day and regain control. And then at the end of the day I would remember that I had chosen a life about going forward and letting go of fear. I would also remember how desperately I wanted drugs and alcohol at the beginning of my abstinence. I felt unsafe in reality, in life – ill equipped to cope emotionally, and very, very unfit.

I also knew that it was worth not giving up, at least giving it a try, as I was curious to know what life would be like without measuring my body's weight for approval every single day, and without having to take the scales on holiday with me or, if that was not possible, reporting back seconds after arriving home, being so desperate for their approval.

I went up two dress sizes within the first three months so that none of my clothes fitted me any more. My pants would not come up over my thighs and my shirts and jackets would no longer do up over my bust. I would become terrified, but underneath the fear was a sense of adventure, for I knew that very few new things in life were easy at the beginning.

I began to watch Nigella Lawson's cooking shows on TV and feel liberated as she spoke so freely about delicious food. I loved the roundness of her body. Mine looked similar – ripe, round breasts, a soft swelling for a belly, full hips – an overall hourglass figure. My waist still remained the smallest part of me. I still had shape; it was just a bigger shape.

I began to shop in the bigger women's stores and came to really enjoy the saleswomen who worked there. I noticed that women who were a little bigger did laugh more. They did not take themselves so seriously. And I still found sexy and professional clothes that were comfortable.

Comfort was such a stranger to me on many levels. These women would chat with me, have a giggle, happily hang up the clothes I discarded and talk about life. They did not try to harass me into buying anything; they understood that I was a grown woman who could choose for myself. I sometimes went into these stores just to be around their jovial energy. They were often women in their fifties who were cheeky but professional: women of substance on every level.

Brad has commented that I have become less inhibited sexually and I laugh more when we make love. I am more adventurous and don't need to keep to the same routine. Oddly I feel safer, more womanly. I have come to like the soft coating that has welcomed itself to my body. I now eat ice cream with Brad and the boys, fish and chips, pizza and chocolate, not just any chocolate, but Swiss chocolate.

Sarah, who works closely with me almost every day, noticed that I am happier and so have the boys. I've caught them smiling at me when they watch me enjoy an ice cream or pizza with them, as it has been such a rare occurrence throughout their lives. I always went without.

The greatest freedom has been that I don't need to binge. I feel so proud that I don't have to sneak food any longer and I don't want to eat as much as I used to. Gone is the urgency to eat as many treats as possible because the next day I would have to diet because I felt so guilty. I can have a chocolate bar in the fridge for a week and just break off a little each night if I feel like it. I am free with my food again because I have choice. Fear removed my ability to choose to give to myself.

I have noticed over the past month or so that my weight has reduced a little as my belts need to be pulled in a notch. I felt oddly empowered speaking to an insurance agent who asked me how much I weighed when completing my medical report. I smiled and said, 'I really don't know; I could be 150 kilograms for all I know.' He smiled back and said, 'You look around 75 kilos to me.'

I have had some new clothes made with elastic waists that can move with me rather than against me as I age. I have noticed grey hairs appearing and the lines around my eyes getting deeper. When I go to the hairdresser I tell her that I don't want my grey covered, that I have earned it. I like these odd silver hairs that are popping up.

I have fought myself all my life – trying to change the essence of who I am because I believed that it was not good enough. I am tired of fighting. Unless I accept all that I am and all that I am not I will not grow into the peaceful, happy woman I choose to be – the woman I see in Barbara's eyes and her mother Mary's eyes. They have fun with their liabilities, they are compassionate towards themselves and they are gracious about their gifts and talents.

The darkness of the denial my life has been shadowed with is leaving as the sunshine of acceptance has begun to warm and heal my heart.

◎ Workout **30**

Accepting acceptance

In an ideal world life would be fair, but today the planet is in far from an ideal state. I must accept that fact today, remembering that acceptance does not mean submission. I don't have to lie down and die and not take action to try to help change some of the problems of our planet. Accepting a fact does not mean that I have to like it – it just means accepting it for today and doing what I can to change what I don't like.

◎ ◎ ◎ ◎ ◎

No-one ever really has their entire why and when questions answered, but if I really want to change how something happens I can find a way. The word 'how' breaks down into the letters H O W which, according to a great man called Bill Wilson, could stand for Honestly, Open-mindedly and Willingly.

◎ ◎ ◎ ◎ ◎

I can make changes to my life today and maybe help another improve their quality of life. How? Honestly, open-mindedly and willingly. If I look honestly at what I don't think is just and let go of the why and the when and just focus on how I can do something to change it, I will find more peace and purpose in my day today. If I open my mind to the myriad of options I could consider and stay open to my dreams, letting go of an investment in a time frame and becoming willing to bring my best effort and attention to the task I find unjust or unfair, it is highly possible that I can begin to make a difference today.

◎ ◎ ◎ ◎ ◎

It has been said that 'happiness is wanting what you have', and that phrase is the best description of acceptance I have ever heard.

◎ ◎ ◎ ◎ ◎

I can make a difference to the world today by:

- choosing to focus on solutions rather than problems
- remembering that I cannot change another but I can change my actions – honestly, open-mindedly and willingly.

8

A final word

I t was only through the reflection of myself in the eyes of my dolphin people that I got to meet myself. They would speak to me in separate conversations, yet echo the same words. Barbara would tell me that I was courageous and brave, attractive and good company, and Brad would echo her words on another day at another time. I believed they saw me; I just couldn't see me in the early days.

When I did finally begin to see myself I was deeply upset. Coming to accept the truth of my childhood and finding the strength to reach out and hold that tiny hand of little Cynthia who I had ignored for decades was almost more than my heart could bear.

I did not want my life to be true. I would have preferred to be a psychopathic liar. And I remember asking my shrink many times if he was sure I was not insane. I wanted to lie about my childhood, and I had for the first 30 years of my life. I lied to myself by pretending it never happened.

I have heard a saying: 'The truth will set you free, but not until it has finished with you.' While I have no idea who said it, I understand it to be true.

The truth is relentless. It will not leave you alone until you face it. You can try to bury it and deny it and escape from it, as I did for decades – or even kill yourself – but I believe if Mother Nature has work for you to do on this planet you cannot fight that.

I watched on the news recently a man throw himself off Niagara Falls and survive. I thought to myself, 'You can't fight Mother Nature; she will not let you leave yet. You have not finished with your truth.'

And then there are those beautiful people who die horrendously or suddenly. I don't understand the workings of the Universe, but I do now understand my own heart a little more and it is my friend.

When I began writing this book months ago I spoke about how I was working on building my own levels of emotional fitness every day.

Emotional fitness is about repetition and consistency – like physical fitness. It's about starting off with what you can handle until you build strength and then taking on a little more – raising the bar.

Writing this book has been for me the hardest emotional triathlon I have ever attempted. I have been comforted and reassured along the way by the written words of many great writers who have shared their experiences about writing from the heart. Erica Jong's words echoed my truth when she said that to 'Tell the truth … you are likely to be a pariah with your family' and Camus reminded me that 'Liberty is the right not to lie.'

Erica Jong's wonderful book, *What do Women Want?*, was one book I was able to get through despite my dyslexia. It was worth the determination and headache I endured, especially when she said on page 178, 'If you are relentlessly honest about what you feel and fear, you often become a mouthpiece for others' feelings as well as your own. People are remarkably similar at the heart level – where it counts. Writers are born to voice what we all feel. That is the gift. And we keep it by giving it away. It is a sacred calling.'

I have sat at my laptop and sobbed – and laughed. My heart has pounded as my truth has involuntarily made its way onto the screen, often without my consent. And once I saw it for myself, I knew that hiding from it was futile, for if I ignore my truth it will just keep presenting itself over and over until I face it. My words are my mouthpiece for my truth.

As I have said earlier, this book has been far more challenging than my first book because I am sharing my own experiences that I was not emotionally strong enough to do three years ago. Some of the stories you have read have actually been part of my advanced workout to write. And I knew as I wrote that I would find empowerment. Writing is a must for me, it is not negotiable. It is as necessary as air and food. It is definitely not a chore and more like 'a sacred calling', as Erica Jong described it. When I write I feel grateful for the honour.

A few days after I sent this manuscript to Sydney bound in ribbon to my publishers for editing, my marriage to Brad ended. We had spent eight years together that were full of love and growth for us both. My desire to write and follow my heart did not help with relieving our financial pressure. It got too much for us both. For me to help relieve the financial pressure and get a job meant letting go of my truth, my charity work, my purpose. I would have become miserable, and Brad was already miserable because carrying the majority of the financial load left him without joy and without a life. He worked like a dog day and night.

Leaving this marriage means going back to a single mother's pension and renting a small until and bringing up my two teenage sons alone. But it also means that nobody else has to bear the financial burden of the life of an author, just me, for this is what my heart chooses.

The love that I shared over the eight years I spent with Brad has empowered me to know myself and to honour myself. Both of my husbands have been remarkable men in their different ways, and I feel blessed to have married them each of them. I have no regrets, and if the only way to arrive at who I am today was to marry them both again, I would – in a blink.

In completing this book I feel like I have both hands in the air as I cross the finishing line. I am tired but elated, smiling but a little sad at the same time. I will miss writing to you. This book has been a companion, a friend to whom I have been talking and now we have to say goodbye. Even though it was a brief love affair, it has taught me a great deal about myself, and isn't that what love is for, to teach us about our own heart?

I have opened my heart and given my all … we both deserve nothing less.

I thank you for being on the other side of these words and taking the journey with me, until next time.

Author's notes

Page 9 'According to one of the most influential writers in this area, Dr Daniel Goleman, emotional intelligence is "the capacity for recognising our own feelings and those of others, for motivating ourselves, and for managing emotions well in ourselves and in our relationships"': Dr Daniel Goleman, *Emotional Intelligence: Why it can matter more than IQ*, Bloomsbury, Great Britain, 1996.

Page 91 'On the trip to London I read Erica Jong's book, *Fear of Flying*': Erica Jong, *Fear of Flying*, Holt, Rinehart and Winston, New York, 1973.

Page 156 '... a statistic released by the Queensland Intravenous Aids Association showed that 92 percent of all intravenous drug addicts had alcoholic parents': This statistic comes from researchers in the In House Detox Department of the Queensland Intravenous Aids Association, Fortitude Valley, Brisbane, 2003.

Page 232 'Erica Jong's words echoed my truth when she said that to "Tell the truth ... you are likely to be a pariah with your family"': Erica Jong, *What do Women Want?*, Bloomsbury, Great Britain, 1999.

Page 232 '... Camus reminded me that "Liberty is the right not to lie"': Quoted in Erica Jong, see above, p. 177.

Page 232 'Erica Jong's wonderful book, *What do women want?*, was one book I was able to get through despite my dyslexia': See above.

Acknowledgements

My first thanks go to my heart's true parent – Mother Nature. I feel your protective love each time I pass beneath a magnificent old tree. When I close my eyes and gently place the cool soft petals of a pink peony rose to my eyelids I feel your kiss. I know your strength when I gaze out at the ocean or watch your magnificence during a thunderstorm. I hear, see and feel you everywhere guiding me, protecting me and picking me up whenever I fall down. I am in awe of you and I love you – thank you for never giving up on me.

I would also like to thank my small but precious heart family. My two beautiful sons, who are now young men: Mitchell and Sam, you light up my life, it's an honour being able to say I am your mother. Thank you for the privilege.

My beautiful Barbara – the matriarch, who holds up the maternal torch when the path of womanhood and motherhood gets tricky, slippery and dark – you have shown me the strength in gentleness. I love you.

My darling Sarah, my soul's sister, what a beautiful and sacred bond we share – thank God for you.

My Pruie, the lavender and vanilla mermaid, my heart lights up every time I see your face. I admire and respect you more than words can ever convey.

And my dear ex-husband, Brad, who taught me so much about myself as a woman.

To Rex Finch and Sean Doyle at Finch Publishing for your belief in this book and me. Your warmth and professional guidance is so deeply appreciated – thank you. To Kathryn Lamberton, who edited this work with an open mind and heart, thank you for the loving spit and polish you gave my words so that readers may see their own reflection in them!

To Dr Timothy Sharp, a special thanks, not just for your professional commentary throughout the book, but for encouraging me to start this project with you – thank you.

To the huge-hearted Emotional Fitness Foundation Board Members, who donate not just their time and professional expertise to building our charity, but also genuine human concern and compassion. Professor John Saunders, Tudor Marsden-Huggins, Robert Morgan, Hal McLauchlan, Sarah Nelson, Barbara Bone, Colleen Watson-O'Brien, Leslie Watson-O'Brien, David Stitt and Jo Plowman – my heartfelt thanks for your tireless support.

To the HADS (Hospital Alcohol & Drug Services) Unit at the Royal Brisbane Hospital, all of the nursing staff and especially to Dean Trevaskis, who treats all the inpatients in the detox with the gentle respect they so desperately need. And to the 4000 inpatients I have run groups for, cried with and held over the past years – my heart is still with you wherever you are.

To my shrink, Dr Malcolm Foxcroft, who over the past seven years has – with his patience, compassion and professionalism – helped me build an amazing life. You are a wonderful human being, Malcolm. Thank you.

And lastly, to my heart's tribe: The Emotional Fitness Team, who volunteer their time to help others learn how to help themselves. I love you all and thank you for the privilege of sharing your journey of recovery. To Sarah Nelson, Prue Andreasson, Ziggy Mitchell, Natalie Campbell, Robert van Mechelen, Steve Humphrey, Lena Lundell, Amerie Davenport, Tim Roy and Ross Woods – you are my heroes and you consistently inspire me to keep moving forward.

What an abundant life. Thank you all.

Contacts

If you have an inquiry about the Emotional Fitness program, please contact Sarah Nelson (seen in the first photo in this book), who is the National Head Facilitator of Emotional Fitness. Her number is 0409 123 994.

Or you can contact Cynthia direct at:

Emotional Fitness
PO Box 2002
Windsor
Queensland. 4030.
cynthia@cynthiamorton.com

To find out more about Cynthia, or to get an update on her activities (including her public speaking engagements), visit her website: www.cynthiamorton.com.

Or contact her agent Hal McLauchlan direct at:

Speakers & Entertainers.Com
Phone: (07) 3849 4448
hal@speakers-entertainers.com.au

To find out more about Dr Tim Sharp and The Happiness Institute, visit these websites:
www.makingchanges.com.au
www.thehappinessinstitute.com

Other Finch titles of interest

Relationships

A Strong Marriage
Staying connected in a world that pulls us apart
Dr William Doherty believes that today's divorce epidemic is the result of overwhelming and conflicting demands on our time, rampant consumerism, and the often skewed emphasis we place on personal fulfilment. This book shows how to restore a marriage worth saving – even when it seems too late. ISBN 1876451 459

Women Can't Hear What Men Don't Say
Destroying myths, creating love
Dr Warren Farrell provides a remarkable communication program to assist couples in understanding and loving each other more fully. ISBN 1876451 319

Side by Side
How to think differently about your relationship
Jo Lamble and Sue Morris provide helpful strategies to overcome the pressures that lead to break-ups, as well as valuable advice on communication, problem-solving and understanding the stages in new and established relationships. A marvellous book for young people. ISBN 1876451 092

Online and Personal
The reality of Internet relationships
With the boom in Internet dating services and chat rooms, the authors, Jo Lamble and Sue Morris, offer guidelines for Net users to protect themselves, their relationships and their children from the hazards that exist online. ISBN 1876451 173

Women's health

Catfight
Why women compete with each other
Leora Tanenbaum explores the roots of destructive competitiveness among women. From diets to dating, from the boardroom to the delivery room, she describes how women compare their looks, bodies, men, career achievements and competence as mothers. These revelations will surprise men and will have women nodding their heads in recognition. ISBN 1876451 491

Your pregnancy
A week-by-week guide to a worry-free pregnancy
Ann Somers
This is an informative, week-by-week guide with whimsical illustrations. Its calendar format provides daily entries for planning and recording the important events of this special time. The perfect gift! ISBN 1876451 36X

Motherhood
Making it work for you
Jo Lamble and Sue Morris provide useful approaches for mothers to deal with difficulties in everyday family life and to help make motherhood a rewarding, enjoyable experience. ISBN 1876451 033

The Body Snatchers
How the media shapes women
Cyndi Tebbel
From childhood, women are told they can never be too thin or too young. The author exposes the rampant conditioning of women and girls by those pushing starvation imagery, and encourages us to challenge society's preoccupation with an ideal body that is unnatural and (for most) unattainable. ISBN 1876451 076

Blood Ties
The stories of five positive women
Edited by Salli Trathen
This collection of the stories of five Australian HIV-positive women reveals how each woman approached her predicament, and the inner qualities she drew on to persevere. The authors' honest and courageous writing allows us to live with them through their struggles. What emerges is a triumph of the human spirit over adversity. ISBN 1 876451 297

Men's health

Manhood
An action plan for changing men's lives (3rd edition)
Steve Biddulph tackles the key areas of a man's life – parenting, love and sexuality, finding meaning in work, and making real friends. He presents new pathways to healing the past and forming true partnerships with women, as well as honouring our own inner needs. ISBN 1876451 203

Stories of Manhood
Journeys into the hidden hearts of men
Steve Biddulph presents his selection of the best writings from around the world on the inner lives of men. Powerful, funny, and heart-rending, these stories show that men are infinitely larger than the narrow stereotypes they are given. ISBN 1876451 106

The Myth of Male Power
Why men are the disposable sex
Dr Warren Farrell presents a significant and well-researched plea against the image of male-as-oppressor, arguing that this misconception has hindered not only men, but women too. ISBN 1876451 300

Dealing with Anger
Self-help solutions for men
Frank Donovan
Focussing on emotional healing and practical change, this book includes case studies from clients of the author's (a psychotherapist) and a program of exercises for the reader. ISBN 1876451 05X

Adult health

Journeys in Healing
How others have triumphed over disease and disability
Dr Shaun Matthews takes us into the lives of eight people who have suffered life-altering illness or disability. Their stories present empowering messages for all sufferers of disease and disability, and demonstrate the interconnectedness between physical, mental, emotional and spiritual health. ISBN 1876451 424

Coping Well
Positive ways to deal with life-challenging disease
Rubin Battino
A practical and sensitive guide for those living with a life-challenging disease and for those caring for them, this book details many effective coping strategies. At its heart is a holistic approach to healing, integrating psychological, spiritual and emotional dimensions. ISBN 1876451 432

Sex-life Solutions
How to solve everyday sexual problems
Respected sex therapist Dr Janet Hall offers clear and practical step-by-step directions for solving all types of sexual difficulties. The book includes sections for men, women, and couples, as well as one on anxieties based on mixed messages and misunderstandings about sex. ISBN 1876451 408

Take Control of Your Life
The five-step plan to health and happiness (2nd edition)
Dr Gail Ratcliffe
This book is a blueprint for recognising what is wrong with your life, minimising your stress and maximising the opportunities to reach your goals. The author, a clinical psychologist, has developed her five-step method of life-planning and stress management with clients for over 13 years. ISBN 1 876451 513

Adolescent health

Boys in Schools
Addressing the real issues – behaviour, values and relationships
Edited by Rollo Browne and Richard Fletcher
Positive accounts of how classroom teachers have implemented innovative approaches to help boys' learning and their understanding of relationships. ISBN 0646239 589

Life Smart
Choices for young people about friendship, family and future
Vicki Bennett
This highly acclaimed book for teenagers provides a valuable perspective and sound advice on how to deal with the most pressing issues of those vital years – the ups and downs of friendship and love, learning to accept ourselves and others, creating a direction in our lives, and relating to our families. ISBN 1876451 130

Girls' Talk
Young women speak their hearts and minds
(Edited by Maria Pallotta-Chiarolli)

Girls want a book that gets real about the issues in their lives. Here 150 young women tell it like it is. A riveting read – credible, direct and heartwarming. ISBN 1876451 025

Children's health

Kids Food Health:
Nutrition and your child's development
The authors, Dr Patricia McVeagh – a paediatrician – and Eve Reed – a dietitian – present the parents of children from newborns to teenagers with the latest information on the impact of diet on health, growth, allergies, behaviour and physical development.
Kids Food Health 1: *The first year* ISBN 1876451 149
Kids Food Health 2: *From toddler to preschooler* ISBN 1876451 157
Kids Food Health 3: *From school-age to teenage* ISBN 1876451 165

Parenting

Baby on Board
Understanding what your baby needs
Dr Howard Chilton provides essential advice and explanations for parents, from the day of birth through the first months of babyhood. This accessible book includes reassuring medical information, a discussion of important issues that require parents' decisions, and a fascinating description of the evolutionary background to the needs of babies. ISBN 1876451 394

Starting School
How to help your child be prepared
Sue Berne
How a child starts off at school plays an important role in determining their approach to education throughout life. This book will help you ensure that your child's practical, emotional and social skills are sufficiently developed to make the most of starting school. ISBN 1 876451 475

Adolescence
A guide for parents
Michael Carr-Gregg and Erin Shale
In this informative and wide-ranging book, the authors help parents understand what is happening for young people aged 10–20 and how to deal with it. They discuss the big questions in a young person's life and provide parents and teachers with useful approaches for handling problems. ISBN 1876451 351

A Handbook for Happy Families
A practical and fun-filled guide to managing children's behaviour
Dr John Irvine
In this wise and humorous approach to parenting, the author tackles the commonest problems with children of all ages. He also presents his innovative and well-tested 'Happy/sad face discipline system', which draws families together rather than dividing them. ISBN 1 876451 416

Raising Boys
Why boys are different – and how to help them become happy and well-balanced men (2nd edition)
In his international bestseller, Steve Biddulph examines the crucial ways that boys differ from girls. He looks at boys' development from birth to manhood and discusses the warm, strong parenting and guidance boys need. ISBN 1 876451 505

Raising Boys Audio
A double-cassette set read by Steve Biddulph. ISBN 1 876451 254

Confident Parenting
How to set limits, be considerate and stay in charge
Dr William Doherty
'We may be the most child-sensitive generations of parents the world has ever known – and the most confused and insecure,' says the author. This book shows you how to parent effectively and how to ensure that your family is not overwhelmed by external pressures such as advertising, TV, and peer culture. ISBN 1876451 467

Parenting after Separation
Making the most of family changes
Jill Burrett
So much parenting now takes place from two households, following separation. This book offers positive approaches to helping children and making the most of these family changes. ISBN 1876451 378

Stepfamily Life
Why it is different – and how to make it work
In this book, Margaret Newman, an experienced couple and family counsellor and a member of a stepfamily herself, describes challenges that members of a stepfamily usually encounter. In her experience, stepfamily life *is* different, and therefore different solutions are needed to get it 'on track' – and, more importantly, to help it survive. Margaret considers a wide range of stepfamily scenarios, and gives practical suggestions as to what to do in each case to overcome any difficulties. ISBN 1876451 521

Father and Child Reunion
How to bring the dads we need to the children we love
Dr Warren Farrell
This book calls for a rejoining of families (and of children with parents who can care for them) by creating equal opportunities for men as parents.
ISBN 1876451 327

Bullybusting
How to help children deal with teasing and bullying
Evelyn Field reveals the 'six secrets of bullybusting', which contain important life skills for any young person. Activities introduce young readers to new skills in communicating feelings, responding to stressful situations and building a support network. An empowering book for parents and their children (5-16 years).
ISBN 1876451 041

On Their Own
Boys growing up underfathered
Rex McCann
For a young man, growing up without an involved father in his life can leave a powerful sense of loss. *On Their Own* considers the needs of young men as they mature, the passage from boyhood to manhood, and the roles of fathers and mothers. ISBN 1876451 084

Fathers After Divorce
Building a new life and becoming a successful separated parent
Michael Green
'Comprehensive, beautifully clear, fair and friendly ... a separated man's best friend.' *Steve Biddulph* ISBN 1876451 009

Fear-free Children
Dr Janet Hall draws on real-life case studies to help parents overcome specific fears and anxieties that their children have, such as fear of the dark, fear of being alone or fear of animals. ISBN 1876451 238

Fight-free Families
Dr Janet Hall provides solutions to conflicts in a wide range of family ages and situations, from young children through to adolescents. ISBN 1876451 22X

Society

Twelve Principles
Living with integrity in the twenty-first century
For a world seeking moral leadership, Tasmanian environmentalist Martin Hawes proposes ways by which we can live responsibly, reappraise our values, and develop a global consciousness. Includes profiles of inspiring people from around the world. ISBN 1876451 483

For further information on these and all of our titles, visit our website:
www.finch.com.au

Index

◎ Personal Progress

Workout –

With respect to this Workout, I was honest about my truth with these people today:

Tertiary person: . . . .

Secondary person: . . . .

Primary person: . . . .

How I feel about it: . . . .
. . . .
. . . .
. . . .
. . . .

How I parented myself: . . . .
. . . .
. . . .
. . . .
. . . .

Ways I would like to improve: . . . .
. . . .
. . . .
. . . .
. . . .
. . . .
. . . .